BOATER'S BOOK OF NAUTICAL TERMS

DAVID S. YETMAN

Editor: John P. Kaufman
Copy Editor: John P. O'Connor, Jr.

BRISTOL FASHION PUBLICATIONS, INC.
Harrisburg, Pennsylvania

Boater's Book Of Nautical Terms

Published by Bristol Fashion Publications, Inc.

ISBN: 1-892216-11-6

LCCN: 98-074351

Contribution acknowledgments

Cover Design: by David S. Yetman & John P. Kaufman.
Inside Graphics: by David S. Yetman.

Boater's Book Of Nautical Terms

INTRODUCTION

During the past several hundred years the boating community has developed a language all its own. This book offers over a thousand examples of nautical terms and phrases from that language. There are many more, some so esoteric that they're used by just a small group. People who are new to the world of boats often have difficulty understanding the meaning of many of the new words to which they are now exposed. Often, it must seem as though they're listening to a language other than English. This book is not intended to list every one of the obscure terms, but I hope it will give the reader an understanding of a broad cross-section of those that may arise in the course of being a boating enthusiast.

Most people use at least a few of these terms or phrases in everyday conversation without realizing the nautical nature of the term. The first entry in this book is a prime example - we are taken *aback* by an unmanageable condition. Sometimes we take a *sounding* to see how much *leeway* we have and grant a *wide berth* to those who may be *off course*. And the phrase "bitter end" takes on a special meaning for anyone who's been unfortunate enough to see the loose end of their anchor rode disappear over the bow and into the deep.

I hope that reading a boating-related magazine or having a conversation on the dock will be much less puzzling after browsing through these pages and that you'll find the book useful as a handy reference even after you've become an old hand.

Enjoy your newfound knowledge.

D. S. Y.

PRONUNCIATION GUIDE

The *Boater's Book of Nautical Terms* provides a pronunciation guide for individual word entries. The phonetic symbols used follow convention except for the *schwa*, which is usually printed as an inverted lower case "e", but for purposes of this informal dictionary is printed as "ĕ".

ā	pāy	ī	sĭt
â	spâre	ī	hīve
ă	căt	î	pîer
ä	fäther	ō	drōve
é	resumé	ô	paw
ě	sět	ŭ	cŭt
ē	bē	û	ûrge
oo	took	ĕ	about, itĕm
oo	boot	'	primary accent
ō	gōt	'	secondary accent

A

aback (ĕ-băk') *adv.* 1. Condition where the clew of a headsail is to windward instead of to leeward of the mast. 2. In an unmanageable condition.

abaft (ĕ-băft') *adv.* 1. Toward the stern. 2. Behind.

abeam (ĕ-bēm') *adv.* To the side, at right angles to the keel of a vessel.

about (ĕ-bout') *adv.* Placing the boat on the opposite tack. (*to go* about *or come* about)

adrift (ĕ-drĭft') *adv.* Without attachment or direction.

aft (ăft) *adv.* Toward, at, in or close to the stern. *-adj.* Located at the stern.

aft cabin 1. An enclosed compartment or living quarters near the stern. 2. A cabin which is behind another.

aground (ĕ-ground') *adv.* On the ground or bottom; stranded by shallow water.

ahull (ĕ-hŭl') *adv.* Said of a sailboat which is drifting with sails furled.

aid to navigation A marker, buoy or landmark which can be used to determine the relative position or proper course of a vessel.

alee (ë-l ë') *adv.* At, on or to the leeward side.

aloft (ë-loft') *adv.* At or in the upper rigging.

alternator (ôl'tër-nā-tër) *n.* An electric generator that produces alternating current (AC).

amidships (ë-mīd'shīps) *adv.* Midway between the bow and the stern.

anchor (ăng'-kër) *n.* A device attached to a vessel by chain or line and cast overboard to keep a vessel from moving, either by its weight, by burying some part of its structure in the sea bed or by snagging some feature of the bottom. *-v.* To secure a vessel with an anchor.

anchor bend A knot of the type used to secure an anchor to its rode.

anchor light A single, white all-around light displayed by a vessel to indicate that it's at anchor.

anchor locker A below-deck compartment in the bow in which the anchor and or its rode may be stowed.

anchorage (ăng'kër-īj) *n.* An area designated or appropriate for anchoring.

anemometer (ăn'--mōm'-ë-tër) *n.* An instrument for measuring wind speed.

angle on the bow (... port bow, ... starboard bow) The angle of your boat's bearing from another, measured from his bow and expressed in degrees, 0 to 180.

anode (ă'nōd) *n.* 1. The positive terminal of a battery. 2. A point of electrical contact. See SACRIFICIAL ANODE.

antifouling paint A coating applied below the waterline of a vessel to discourage marine growth on the treated surface.

apparent wind The combination of true wind and wind caused by motion of the vessel.

aspect ratio The ratio of a sail's luff (height) to its foot (width).

astronomical tide See SPRING TIDE.

athwart (ë-thwôrt') *adv.* Positioned on a port-to-starboard axis. (*also*, athwartships)

ATON See AID TO NAVIGATION.

autopilot (ô'tō-pī'-lë t) *n.* A device that automatically steers a vessel on a prescribed course.

auxiliary (ôg'zīl'ër-ē) n. 1. A sailboat's engine. 2. A sailboat equipped with an engine.

avast (ë-văst') *interj.* A command to desist.

awash (ë-wôsh') *adv.* 1. At or near water level. 2. Close enough to the surface to cause waves to break above it.

aweigh (ë-wā') *adv.* Said of an anchor that's been raised (weighed) clear of the bottom.

azimuth (ăz'ĕ-mĕth') *n*. A direction expressed as an angle clockwise from North.

B

back (băk) *v.* To change direction counterclockwise (*said of the wind*). Compare VEER.

backplate (Also Backer Plate) A metal reinforcement placed behind a panel or bulkhead to prevent through-bolted hardware from being pulled out.

backstay (băk'stā) *n.* A structural line or cable, part of the standing rigging, connecting the top of a mast to the stern.

backwash See WASH.

backwinded (băk'wīn'dĕd) *adj.* Where the wind is deflected from one sail into the lee of another.

baggywrinkle (băg'ē-rīnk'-ĕl) *n.* Chafing gear wrapped around shrouds to protect sails from abrasion.

Bahamian mooring Two bow anchors positioned 180 degrees apart.

bail[1] (bāl) *v.* 1. To remove water from a boat by means of filling a container and emptying it over the side. 2. To empty a boat by this method.

bail[(2)] (bāl) *n.* The arched handle of a container such as a pail.

bait station An onboard site for the preparation of bait for fishing.

baitwell (bāt'wĕl) *n.* A built-in container for storing bait on board a vessel.

ball cock (*also* ball valve) A valve whose shutoff mechanism is a rotating ball with a hole through it. It is opened by turning the ball to align its through-hole with the intake and outlet ports.

ballast (băl'ĕst) *n.* Heavy material placed in or attached to a vessel to improve stability. -*v.* To stabilize with or provide such material.

ballast keel A blade-shaped projection suspended from the keel to place ballast below the hull.

balsa core A layer of balsa wood laminated between two thin, durable outer layers to form a light, strong structural unit.

bar (bär) *n.* A sandy shoal; sandbar.

bare poles Said of a sailboat with no sails deployed.

bareboat (bâr'bōt) *n.* An un-crewed vessel. -*adj* Without crew. *(Said of a chartered or rented boat)*

barge (bärj) *n.* An unpowered vessel for the transportation of bulk goods, usually towed or pushed by a tugboat.

bark (bärk) *n.* (*also,* barque) A sailing vessel with three to five masts, all of them square-rigged except the after mast which is fore-to-aft rigged.

barkentine (bär'kĕn-tēn') *n.* A sailing vessel with three to five masts, of which only the foremast is square-rigged, the others being fore-to-aft rigged.

barometer (bär-ōm'ĕ-tĕr) *n.* An instrument for measuring atmospheric pressure.

bass boat 1. A small, flat-bottomed, outboard-powered boat with platforms or seats for anglers. 2. An open powerboat with flush foredeck and a small cuddy cabin.

bateau (bă-tō') *n.* A small, flat-bottomed boat, tapered at both ends; common in Louisiana and French Canada.

batten (băt'n) *n.* A strip of semi-rigid material inserted into the pocket of a sail to control its shape.

batten down To secure or make fast (*in anticipation of rough weather*).

beach (bēch) *v.* To haul or drive a vessel ashore. *-n.* A sandy shore.

beacon (bēk'n) *n.* A highly visible landmark or aid to navigation, usually lighted.

beam (bēm) *n.* 1. The width of a vessel at its widest point. 2. A structural frame member athwartships, usually to support the deck.

beam reach Sailing with the apparent wind abeam.

beam sea Wave motion coming in at right angles to the vessel's keel.

bear (bâr) *v.* To proceed in a specific direction.

bear down To approach from windward.

bear off (also fall off, head off, pay off) To alter course, especially away from the wind.

bearing (bāër'ing) *n.* Direction relative to North or relative to the heading of the boat.

beating (bē'tīng) *v.* Sailing into the wind.

Beaufort scale A scale in which the force of the wind is expressed as numbers from 0 (calm) to 12 (hurricane). See Table 1.

becalm (bī-käm') *v.* To render motionless for a lack of wind.

becket (běk'ët) *n.* A line, strap or other device used to hold a line or spar in position.

becket hitch A knot used to tie lines of unequal diameter together.

before the wind Sailing with the wind directly abaft.

belay (bë-lā') *v.* 1. To make fast (a line, for example) to a cleat or pin. 2. To cause to stop.

belaying pin A removable pin or dowel used to make running rigging fast.

bell (běl) *n.* A device which emits a tone when struck.

bell buoy An aid to navigation affixed with a bell or gong which is rung by wave motion.

BEAUFORT SCALE

Beaufort number or force	Wind speed (knots)	Description	Effect
0	under 1	Calm	Sea like a mirror
1	1 - 3	Light air	Small ripples
2	4 - 6	Light breeze	Short, small pronounced wavelets with no crests
3	7 - 10	Gentle breeze	Large wavelets (2 feet high) with some crests
4	11 - 16	Moderate breeze	Small waves (4 feet high) becoming longer, with some whitecaps (foam crests)
5	17 - 21	Fresh breeze	Moderate lengthening waves (6 feet high) with many whitecaps and chance of spray
6	22 - 27	Strong breeze	Large waves (10 feet high) with extensive whitecaps and some spray
7	28 - 33	Near gale	Sea piles up; white foam from breaking waves (14 feet high) begins to be blown in streaks
8	34 - 40	Gale	Moderately high waves (18 feet) of greater length; edges of crests break into spindrift (heavy spray); foam is blown in well marked streaks
9	41 - 47	Strong gale	High waves (23 feet); dense foam streaks; crests begin to roll over; spray reduces visibility
10	48 - 55	Storm	Very high waves (29 feet) with long, overhanging crests; sea begins to look white, visibility is greatly reduced and the rolling of the sea becomes heavy and shock-like
11	56 - 63	Violent storm	Exceptionally high waves (37 feet) that may obscure medium-sized vessels; all wave crests blown into froth; sea covered with patches of white foam
12	64 and greater	Hurricane	Air filled with foam and spray; waves 45 feet and over; sea completely white

Table 1

below (bë-lō') *adv.* Beneath the deck.

bend (bĕnd) *n.* A knot which fastens one line to another. *-v.* To attach a sail to a spar.

berth (bûrth) *n.* 1. A built-in bed or other place to sleep. 2. A space at a wharf for a boat to dock. *-v.* To bring a boat to dock.

bight (bīt) *n.* 1. A loop in a line on which a knot will be formed. 2. A bay formed by the curvature of the shore.

bilge (bīlj) *n.* The area within a hull below the cabin sole.

bilge blower An electric fan used to exhaust dangerous vapors from the bilge.

bilge keels Small keels on either side of the main keel to provide stability, especially in resistance to rolling.

bilge pump A manual or electrically powered device for draining water that accumulates in the bilge and pumping it overboard.

bimini (bī'mī-nē) *n.* A fabric shade mounted above the helm or cockpit to protect the occupants from sun and rain.

binnacle (bīn'ë-kël) *n.* An enclosure in which a compass is mounted.

bitt (*also,* **bit**) (bīt) *n.* A heavy and firmly mounted device to which lines are secured. See Figure 2.

bitter end The unfastened end of a line, chain or rode.

blanket (blăng'kĭt) *v.* To prevent a sail from getting wind by obstructing the wind with another object such as the sail of another vessel.

block (blŏk) *n.* A case enclosing one or more sheaves and having a hook, eye or strap by which it may be attached. See SHEAVE.

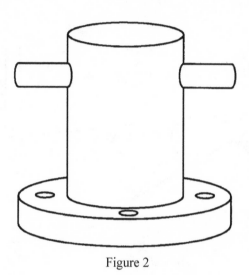

Figure 2

Bitt

bluff bow A blunt, buoyant bow.

boat (bōt) *n.* A waterborne vessel, usually under 65 feet (20m) in length. See SHIP.

boatel (bō-tĕl') *n.* (*informal*) A hotel that provides dockage for guest's boats.

boathook (bōt'hook) *n.* A long handle affixed with a hook and a spike, used to grapple or push off from distant objects.

boatswain (*also* **bos'n** *or* **bosun**) (bō'sĕn) *n.* A crew member in charge of lines and rigging.

boatwright (bōt'rīt) n. A person skilled in the manufacture or maintenance of boats (*esp. wooden*).

bobstay (bôb'stā) *n.* A line or cable running from the lower stem to the bowsprit, counteracting the pull from forestay. See Figure 3.

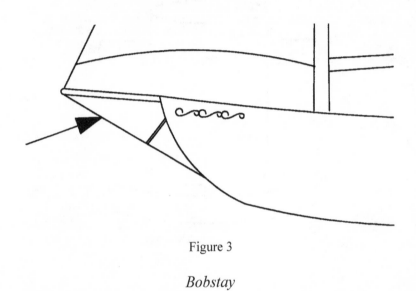

Figure 3

Bobstay

bold shore A steep shore by deep water.

bollard (bôl'ĕrd) *n.* A heavy post at the edge of a wharf, to which lines may be made fast.

bolster (bōl'stĕr) *n.* A padded cushion at the side of a seat or around a coaming.

boltrope (bōlt'rōp) *n.* A reinforcing line along the edge of a sail.

boom (b<u>oo</u>m) *n.* 1. A spar extending from a mast to hold the foot of a sail. 2. A string of floating objects used to contain spillage, logs or debris floating in the water.

boom crutch (*also* **boom crotch**) A notched support for the main boom when the sail is lowered.

boom vang See VANG.

boomkin (*also* **bumpkin**) (b<u>oo</u>m'kīn, bŭmp'kīn) *n.* 1. A spar extending over the side. 2. A spar extending from the stern to support the backstay.

boot top A line painted around the topsides just above the waterline.

bore (bôr) *n.* A high wave caused by a flood tide in a restricted passage or by colliding tidal currents.

bosun See BOATSWAIN

bosun's chair A seat or harness with an attachment point for a line, used to hoist a crew member into the rigging aloft.

bottlescrew See TURNBUCKLE.

bottom paint See ANTI-FOULING PAINT.

bow (bou) *n.* The front section of a vessel.

bow eye A circular or "U"-shaped attachment point, usually bolted through the stem and used in hauling, towing or mooring a boat.

bow line A line made fast to a bitt or cleat at or near the bow.

bow pulpit A narrow extension of the deck out over the bow.

bow rail An elevated safety rail around the perimeter of the forward deck.

bow rider A runabout with seating in its open bow.

bow roller A horizontal spool in (or at the forward lip of) the bow pulpit over which the anchor rode rides.

bow thruster A reversible, electrically or hydraulically powered propeller mounted in an athwartships tunnel just below the waterline at the bow; used to enhance slow-speed maneuverability by providing a sideward thrust during docking or turning. See Figure 4.

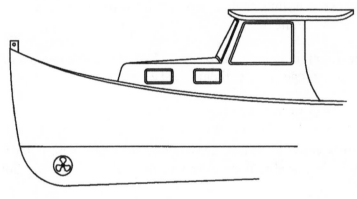

Figure 4

Bow Thruster

bow wave Water which is displaced by a vessel's bow during forward motion at displacement speeds.

bowline (bō'l ën) *n.* 1. A knot which forms a loop that won't slip. 2. A line leading forward from the leech of a square sail.

bowsprit (bou'sprīt) *n.* A spar extending forward from the stem of a vessel to which the forestay may be fastened.

break out To remove from storage in preparation for use.

breaker (brā'kër) *n.* A wave whose crest topples over when it becomes unstable due to its height or shoals beneath.

breakwater (brāk'wôt'ër) *n.* A natural or man-made barrier which provides protection from the open sea.

breast hook A reinforcing member at the joint between the stem and the keel of a wooden vessel.

breast line A dock line which leads directly abeam.

bridge (brĭj) *n.* An elevated helm station on larger vessels.

bridge deck 1. The raised area of an open boat between the cockpit and the companionway. 2. The level on which the helm is located.

bridle (brī'dël) *n.* A line which is fastened to multiple cleats or looped around the hull to safely distribute the stresses induced during towing. The tow line is then made fast to the bridle.

brig (brĭg) *n.* A two-masted sailing ship, square-rigged on both masts, having two or more headsails and a gaff sail or spanker aft of the mizzenmast. 2. A naval jail.

brigantine (brĭg'ën-tēn') *n.* A two-masted sailing ship, square-rigged on the foremast and having a fore-and-aft mainsail with square main topsails.

bright work Varnished wood trim or joinery.
bristol (brĭs'tël) *adj.* Perfectly maintained in first-class condition; pristine. *(said of a boat)*

bristol-fashion The highest standard of condition to which any vessel can be maintained. The highest level of seamanship an individual or crew can attain.

broach (brōch) *v.* To veer broadside to the wind or waves, subjecting the boat to possible capsizing.

broad on the beam A direction at right angles to the keel; abeam.

broad on the bow A direction midway between abeam and dead ahead.

broad on the quarter A direction midway between abeam and dead astern.

broad reach Sailing with the apparent wind on the quarter.

bulkhead (bŭlk'hĕd) *n.* A vertical partition dividing a vessel into compartments.

bulwark (bŭl'wĕrk) *n.* 1. The part of a vessel's side which extends above the deck. 2. A raised lip at the edge of a deck.

bumboat (bŭm'bōt) *n* . A small boat used to peddle goods to visiting vessels in port.

bung (bŭng) *n.* A stopper to fit in a hole, especially in a keg or cask.

bunt (bŭnt) *n.* The excess material resulting from the partial reefing of a sail.

buoy (boo'ē, boi) *n.* A tethered, floating aid to navigation. -*v.* To keep afloat.

buoyancy (boi'ĕn-cē') *n.* The ability to float in a liquid or in air.

butterfly (bŭt'tĕr-flī) *adv.* Running before the wind with the mainsail and the jib set on opposite sides of the boat.

by the wind See CLOSE HAULED.

C

cabin (kǎ'bīn) *n.* An enclosed compartment on a vessel serving as shelter or living quarters.

camber (kǎm'bër) *n.* The convex curve of a deck.

can (kǎn) *n.* A cylindrical, green, odd-numbered buoy.

canoe (cë-noo') *n.* A light, narrow boat with raised, identically pointed bow and stern.

canoe stern A pointed stern having no transom. (*as seen on a double-ender*)

cant (kǎnt) *n.* A frame or rib of a hull that leans fore or aft.

canvas (kǎn'vës) *n.* 1. A heavy, coarse, tightly woven cloth, usually made of cotton. 2. The general term for fabrics of all types used for boat enclosures and covers. 3. Covers, enclosures or sails made from such materials.

capacity plate A label or stamped plate which describes a vessel's maximum approved load.

capsize (kǎp-sīz') *v.* To turn over or cause to turn over.

capstan (căp'stăn) *n.* A winch whose drum rotates on a vertical axis.

caravel or **caravelle** (kăr'ă-věl') (*also* **carvel** [kär 'v-l]) *n.* A small, light, 16th & 17th century sailing ship.

careen (că-rēn') *v.* To heel a boat over, usually on a beach, to perform maintenance or repairs.

carlin (kăr'lĕn) *n.* A longitudal reinforcing member between deck beams on a wooden vessel.

carry away To cause to break away or part.

carvel planked A construction method in which the wooden planks of a hull are laid next to one another and made watertight by forcing caulking into the seam between them. See OAKUM.

cast off To release mooring or dock lines and get under way.

cat (kăt) *n.* A catamaran or catboat.

cat boat A sailboat carrying a single sail on a mast stepped well forward.

cat rig See CATBOAT.

cat's paw The ripples on the surface of the water caused by a light breeze.

catamaran (kăt'ĕ-mĕ-răn') *n.* A boat with two parallel hulls which are identical or mirror images of each other. See OUTRIGGER. See Figure 6.

cathead (kăt'hĕd) *n.* A beam projecting from the bow of a vessel, used as a support to lift the anchor.

cathedral hull A V-hull with prominent, concave chines (*also called a* tri-hull). See Figure 7.

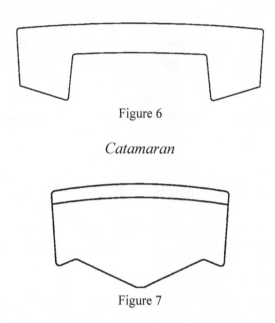

Figure 6

Catamaran

Figure 7

Cathedral or Reverse Chine

catwalk (kăt'wôk) *n.* 1. A finger pier. 2. A raised walkway.

caulk (kôk) *v.* To seal by filling the space between two things, especially the seams between hull planks or strakes.

cavitation (kăv'ë-tă'shën) *n.* A condition where a damaged or overdriven propeller causes the surrounding water to break down into a gas, impeding performance and eventually damaging the prop.

ceiling (sē'līng) *n.* The inner finishing layer of a wooden hull, usually light wood or slats.

celestial navigation A method of determining position relative to pre-calculated positions of heavenly bodies.

center cockpit A cockpit located midway between the bow and the stern.

center console 1. A small, raised control station in an open boat, with walkways on both sides. 2. A boat with such a feature.

center of effort The theoretical central point of wind pressure on all sail being carried.

centerboard (cĕn'tër-bōrd') *n.* A small, hinged keel, usually on a sailboat, which may be raised or lowered.

chafing gear Devices such as sleeves, fitted to mooring or dock lines to protect them from wear caused by wave or tidal motion.

chain (chān) *n.* A flexible series of interconnected oblong metal links, primarily used as anchor rode on boats.

chain locker See ANCHOR LOCKER.

chain plate Mounting point where a sailboat's shrouds are attached to the deck or hull.

chandlery (chănd'lë-rē) *n.* A store which sells supplies and provisions for the marine trade.

chart (chärt) *n.* A nautical map which shows latitude and longitude, the topography of the seabed, shoreline features and aids to navigation.

chart plotter   An electronic instrument which displays navigation charts and information on a screen.

chebacco (shĕ-băk'ō) *n.* A small, two-masted, double-ended fishing boat built in the Massachusetts area during the 18th century.

check valve An in-line valve that permits flow in one direction only.

cheek block A block which is mounted against a spar or flat surface.

chine (chīn) *n.* The intersection of the hull and sides on a flat or v-bottomed boat; said to be *hard* (sharp-cornered) or *soft* (rounded).

chock (chôk) *n.* A guide through which lines are led. See Figure 8.

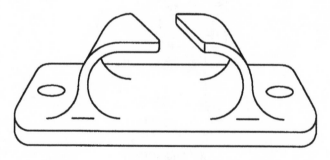

Figure 8

Chock

chop (chôp) *n.* Closely spaced, wind-driven waves.

chum (chŭm) *n.* Minced fish or fish parts introduced to the water to attract predatory game fish to the vicinity.

chute (sho͞ot) *n.* A spinnaker.

cigarette boat A long, narrow, high-powered speedboat.

clamp (klămp) *n.* A longitudal support at the intersection of the deck and topsides or along the gunwales (*also called a* sheer clamp).

cleat (klēt) *n.* A fitting, often in the shape of an anvil, to which lines are made fast. See BITT and SAMSON POST. See Figure 9

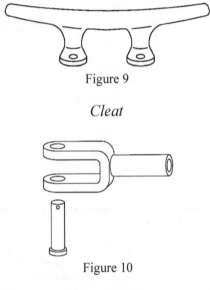

Figure 9

Cleat

Figure 10

Clevis Fitting

cleaver propeller A high performance propeller designed to be operated with only its lower half in the water.

clevis (klĕv'ĭs) *n.* A "Y"-shaped metal fitting with holes through which a pin is inserted to secure it to a tab or other connector. See Figure 10.

clew (kl<u>oo</u>) *n*. 1. The lower aft corner of a sail. 2. Either lower corner of a square sail.

clinker (klĭng'kẽr) *adj*. (Usually clinker-built) A method of constructing a hull with overlapping strakes which are fastened to each other. Lapstrake.

clinometer (klī'nŏm'ĭ-tẽr) *n*. An instrument for measuring the heel angle of a sailboat.

clipper (klĭp'ẽr) *n*. A sharp-bowed, high-masted 18th century sailing vessel built for great speed.

clipper bow A sharp, forward-arching bow.

close aboard Near, but not on a vessel.

close reach Sailing hard into the wind.

close-hauled A point of sailing where the sheets are hauled tight so the boat can sail against the wind.

club-footed jib A small jib with a boom attached to its foot.

coaming (kō'mĭng) *n*. A short, vertical wall around a cockpit or hatch to keep water out.

coble (kô'bël) *n*. A small fishing boat with a lug sail, common in northeast England.

cockboat (kôk'bōt) (*archaic*) *n*. A small rowboat used as a tender.

cockpit (kôk'pĭt) *n*. 1. A recessed opening in the deck for the helm station. 2. An open area, usually aft, often for fishing.

cockpit motor yacht A yacht with a cockpit aft on the main deck.

cold-molded Bonded, laminated or impregnated with polyester or epoxy resins which do not require added heat to cure.

COLREGS (The International Regulations for Preventing Collisions at Sea, 1972) Rules of the nautical road governing vessels operating on the high seas. Compare INLAND NAVIGATIONAL RULES.

come about To change the direction of a tack.

commission (kë-mīsh'ën) *v.* 1. To put a vessel into service. 2. To place an order for the construction of a vessel.

commuter (kë-myoo'tër) *n.* A fast, comfortable, often luxurious dayboat for travel between home and work.

companionway (kôm-păn'yën-wā ') *n.* A stairway or entrance leading below to a cabin

compartment (kôm-pärt'mĕnt) *n.* A space below enclosed by bulkheads.

compass (kŭm'păs) *n.* 1. A navigation instrument used to determine geographical direction, fitted with a pivoting, magnetized indicator needle, dome or card which always aligns itself with the earth's magnetic field. 2. An electronic navigational instrument which uses the output from a sensor (flux gate) to compute its relationship to the earth's magnetic field and display the result on a digital readout.

compass rose A circular detail on a chart showing its orientation to True North and Magnetic North (and the variation between them) and providing a printed protractor for determining bearings.

composite (kôm'pôz'ĭt) *n.* A material made up of two or more different components, such as fiber-reinforced plastic (*usually reserved for combinations of exotic components*).

compression post A support between the heel of a deck-mounted mast and the keel.

convertible (kôn-vĕr'të-bël) *n.* A cruiser with a small salon at cockpit level, forward accommodations below and a fly bridge; often rigged for fishing.

coracle (kôr'ë-kël) *n.* A small boat constructed from animal skins stretched over a wooden frame.

cordage (kôr'dĭj) *n.* Ropes, twine and string.

corvette (kôr-vĕt') *n.* 1. A sailing warship with a single tier of guns. 2. A small, fast warship used mainly for convoy protection.

counter (koun'tër) *n.* The underside of a hull's aft overhang.

counter stern A stern whose transom is above the water line.

counter-rotation Turning in opposite directions. Usually refers to propellers on separate shafts turning in opposite directions to neutralize the effect of prop-walk. Compare DUAL PROPELLER.

course (kôrs) *n.* The route on which a vessel is steered. See BEARING and HEADING.

cove stripe A decorative stripe painted along a boat's sheer.

covering boards   The protective or decorative layer (usually wood) on the top surface of the gunwale.

cowl   (koul)   *n.* A scoop or funnel for ventilation intake or exhaust. See DORADE.

coxswain   (kôk'sën, -swān)   *n.* A person who steers the boat or racing shell and directs the crew.

cradle   (krā'dël)   *n.* A structure used to support a vessel while it's out of the water.

craft   (krăft)   *n.* Any waterborne conveyance, without regard to size.

cribbing   (krīb'īng)   *n.* Large blocks of wood used to support the boat's hull during dry storage.

cringle   (krīng'ël)   *n.* A reinforcing ring sewn into a sail so a line can pass (reef cringle).

crosstree   (krôs'trē)   *n.* A crosspiece on a mast, used to spread the shrouds. Spreader.

crown   (kroun)   *n.* The area of an anchor, opposite the eye, where the shank meets the stock.

crow's nest   A lookout station aloft.

cruiser   (kroo'zër)   *n.* A vessel which is rigged primarily for comfortable life aboard.

cuddy   (kŭ'dē)   *n.* A sheltered area or cabin toward the bow of a small boat.

cunningham   (kŭn'nīng'hăm)   *n.* A line which is used to move the draft of a sail forward or aft .

cup (kŭp) *n.* The curved trailing edge of a propeller blade.

currach (kûr' ĕkh) See CORACLE

current (kŭr'rĕnt) *n.* The horizontal movement of air or water.

Cutlass Bearing® A rubber tube that is sized to a propeller shaft and which fits inside the propeller shaft strut on an inboard engine boat.

cutter (kŭt'ĕr) *n.* 1. A single-masted, fore-and-aft-rigged sailing vessel with a mainsail and two headsails. 2. A small, fast powerboat, such as used by the Coast Guard.

D

daggerboard (dăg'r-bôrd) *n.* A keel which is raised or lowered vertically, rather than hinged. Compare CENTER-BOARD.

Danforth (dăn'fôrth) *n.* A type of stockless anchor with pivoting flukes on its arm.

davit (dăv'ĕt) *n.* An onboard crane or arm which is fitted with a device, such as a block and tackle, for lifting and storing a smaller boat aboard.

day beacon An unlighted aid to navigation, usually a daymark on a piling.

day boat A boat which lacks long-term living accommodations.

day sailer A small sailboat lacking long-term living accommodations.

day shape A geometrically shaped marker, such as a ball, cone or cylinder hung aloft to indicate a vessel's type, occupation or state. (*ex: One black ball displayed means "anchored"; three black balls mean "aground."*)

daymark (dā'märk) *n.* A signboard of specific shape, which, when mounted on a piling, becomes a day beacon.

dead in the water Making no way, but not anchored, moored, tied up or aground.

dead reckoning Navigation method by which position is calculated from course steered and velocity made good.

dead run Running before the wind.

deadeye (dĕd'ī) *n.* A guide through which shrouds or other lines are led.

deadhead (dĕd'hĕd) *n.* A log or beam which has become so waterlogged that it floats just beneath the surface.

deadlight (dĕd'līt) *n.* A fixed skylight or non-opening port.

deadrise (dĕd'rīz') *n.* The angle at which a v-hull's bottom rises from the keel to the chines.

deck (dĕk) *n.* The horizontal platform which encloses a vessel's hull.

deckboat See PONTOON BOAT.

deckhead (dĕk'hĕd) *n.* The finished underside of a cabin or compartment roof; what would be called a ceiling ashore.

deckhouse (dĕk'hous) *n.* A cabin on a vessel's deck. See PILOTHOUSE.

deep six (*informal*) To discard overboard.

deep V hull Generally, a hull with a deadrise angle greater than 19 degrees at the stern. See Figure 11.

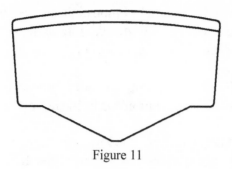

Figure 11

Deep V Planning Hull (25°)

delaminate (dē'lăm'ë-nāt) *v.* To separate from an adjacent layer or surface to which there was a structural attachment. (*often , in boats, the result of moisture seeping into fiberglass by osmosis.*)

demarcation line The charted delineation between areas falling under COLREGS and Inland Navigation Rules.

depth sounder A device which measures the depth of the water by calculating the delay between transmitted and received sound waves reflected off the bottom by a transducer.

deviation (dē'vē-ā'shën) *n.* 1. Compass error caused by onboard conditions; the difference between indicated and magnetic North.

dew point The temperature at which air becomes saturated and releases its moisture in the form of droplets (fog).

dhow (dhou) *n.* An evolved form of lateen-rigged sailing vessel of the Arabian area.

diesel (dē'zël) *n.* 1. A diesel engine. 2. A boat powered by a diesel engine.

43

Diesel engine An internal combustion engine which uses the heat caused by extreme compression to ignite its fuel charge on each firing stroke.

dieseling (dē'zĕl-īng') *n.* Unintended run-on of a non-diesel engine after its ignition has been shut off.

differential GPS (*often*, **DGPS**) A system which uses the signal from a shore-based transmitter to compensate for reduced resolution during selective availability of the GPS system. See SELECTIVE AVAILABILITY.

dinghy (dīng'ē) *n.* A small boat used by another as a life boat or tender.

dismast (dīs-măst') *v.* To (disastrously) carry away the mast.

displacement (dīs-plăs'mĕnt) *n.* The weight of the water displaced by a floating hull.

displacement hull A hull shape which moves through the water while in motion and is supported only by its buoyancy . Compare PLANING HULL. See Figure 12.

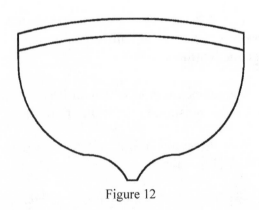

Figure 12

Displacement Hull

displacement speed The speed at which a hull travels through the water without relying on a planing effect. See HULL SPEED.

ditty bag A small sack for personal gear.

dividers (dī-vī'dërs) *n.* A navigation tool comprised of two pointed shafts joined at a pivot and used to determine distances on a chart.

dock (dôk) *n.* 1. The space between two piers used to berth a vessel. 2. A pier or wharf. -v. To bring a vessel to a pier or wharf to tie up.

dockage (dôk'ëj) *n.* Space or tie-up facilities provided for a vessel.

dodger (dôj'ër) n. A cockpit windscreen mounted at the aft edge of a sailboat's cabin. See Figure 13.

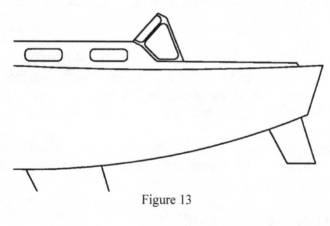

Figure 13

Dodger

dogbody (dôg'bôd-ē) *n.* An 18th Century, two-masted New England fishing boat, essentially a pinky with a square stern. See PINKY and CHEBACCO.

45

doghouse (dôg'hous) *n.* A low deckhouse.

dolphin (dôl'fĕn) *n.* A group of piles tied together for use as a mooring or channel marker.

dolphin striker See MARTINGALE.

dorade (dō'rād) *n.* A ventilating scoop provided with a baffled chamber which prevents water from entering along with the air.

dory (dôr'ē) *n.* A narrow, flat-bottomed boat with high sides and a sharp bow.

double-ender (dŭb'ĕl-ĕn'dër) *n.* A vessel whose bow and stern are pointed.

Down East Traditional name for eastern coastal Maine.

down rigger A device used to keep fishing tackle at a specific depth.

draft (drăft) *n.* 1. The distance from the waterline to the lowest part of a vessel's keel or propulsion equipment. 2. The depth of water required to keep a vessel afloat. (*A vessel is said to* draw *3 feet [its draft].*)

dragger (drâ'gër) n. A commercial vessel which fishes by dragging its equipment along the bottom. Compare SEINER.

drain tide See NEAP TIDE.

draw See DRAFT.

dredge (drej) *n.* 1. A net or scoop dragged along the seabed to capture marine life. 2. A device for removing material from the seabed. 3. A barge equipped with such a device. *-v.* 1. To remove material from the seabed. 2. To enlarge or deepen a channel.

drogue (drōg) *n.* A device, often parachute-shaped, which is lowered into the water and hauled behind a vessel to retard, but not stop its forward motion and provide directional stability during heavy weather. Compare SEA ANCHOR.

dry rot Decay in wood caused by intrusive moisture, especially after it has dried out.

dry stack An arrangement which routs an engine's exhaust directly up through the deck (and cabin) rather than back through the cooling water outlet (*often seen on fishing or lobster boats*).

drysail (drī'sāl) *v.* To store a vessel out of the water.

dual propeller A drive mechanism which uses two counter-rotating propellers on coaxial shafts to increase the efficiency of an outdrive unit or outboard motor.

dual station Having helm stations at two locations, usually in the salon and on the flybridge.

E

earing (*also,* **earring**) (ēr'ring) *n.* A line secured to a cringle, used to bend or reef a sail.

ebb (ĕb) *n.* The outgoing phase of a tide. *-v.* 1. To go out. 2. To ease or reduce.

EFI See ELECTRONIC FUEL INJECTION.

electrolysis (ë-lĕk'trôl'ë-sës) *n.* The potentially destructive galvanic interaction that results from electrically conducting metals being immersed in a liquid. See SACRIFICIAL ANODE.

electronic fuel injection (**EFI**) The control of a fuel injection system by electronic means, such as a microprocessor, rather than mechanical. See FUEL INJECTION.

emergency position indicating radio beacon (EPIRB) A floating transmitter whose position is detected by shore- or satellite-based receivers and relayed to search and rescue facilities.

enclosure (ĕn-klō'zhŭr) *n.* A fabric convertible top with side and rear curtains.

ensign (ĕn'sën) *n.* 1. A national flag displayed on a vessel. 2. The lowest-ranking commissioned officer in the U.S. Navy or Coast Guard.

entry (ĕn'trē) *n.* 1. The way a bow interacts with the water when under way. 2. The shape of the bow; said to be fine or bluff.

EPIRB See EMERGENCY POSITION INDICATING RADIO BEACON.

epoxy (ë-pôx'ē) *n.* A liquid resin which polymerizes into a solid when mixed with a catalyst.

equal interval light A lighted aid to navigation whose "on" time period and "off" time period are equal in length.

even keel (*usually*, on an even keel) Proceeding uneventfully; smoothly.

express cruiser (*also*, **express fisherman**) A fast, usually open boat with direct cockpit access from the helm and overnight accommodations in a forward cabin below.

extended deck motor yacht A sedan cruiser whose upper deck extends aft to cover and often enclose the main deck.

eye of the wind The direction from which the wind is coming.

eye splice A junction formed by weaving the end of a line back into the standing part, creating a loop in the end of the line.

F

fag end The end of a line that has frayed or unraveled.

fair (fâr) *adj.* 1. Describing an area or feature which leads into its adjoining area or features smoothly and harmoniously. 2. Describing a line, arc or curve which follows an intended course without localized deviations. -*v.* 1. To eliminate irregularities in a line, arc or plane. 2. To make smooth or regular by adding or removing material.

fairlead (fâr'lēd) *n.* A chock or guide through which line is led.

fairway (fâr'wā) *n.* A channel for boats in restricted areas, such as between rows of finger piers.

fake (f āk) *n.* A layer or loop of a line that is stacked or coiled to facilitate fast run-off. -*v.* *(Usually with* down, *ie:* faked down) To stow a line in such a fashion. Compare FLEMISH.

fall (fôl) *n.* The part of a tackle which is hauled upon.

falling off Changing course to sail away from the wind. Compare HEADING UP.

fantail (făn'tāl) *n.* A stern that is rounded (*as viewed from above*).

fast (făst) *adv.* (*usually* to make fast) Securely attached.

fathom (făth'ĕm) *n.* A unit of linear measurement equal to six feet.

favor (fā'v-ĕr) *v.* Stay closer to.

feather (fĕth'ĕr) *v.* 1. To turn an oar blade horizontal at the end of a stroke. 2. To blend in the edge of a repair or **seam**. See FAIR.

felucca (fĕ-loo'kĕ) *n.* A narrow, fast vessel propelled by oars or lateen sails; common in the Mediterranean.

fend off To prevent contact between two objects.

fender (fĕnd'ĕr) *n.* A cushion hung on the side of vessel to prevent contact with another object such as a dock or vessel.

fetch (fĕtch) *n.* The distance a wave travels free of obstructions. *-v.* To extend a windward run without tacking.

fiberglass (*also*, **fibreglass**) (fī'b-r-glăs') *n.* 1. Glass which has been spun into fine, flexible threads. 2. Mats or cloth manufactured from fiberglass. 3. The rigid material (fiberglass-reinforced-plastic or FRP) which results from impregnating fiberglass with a resin which hardens during the manufacturing process.

fid See MARLINSPIKE.

fiddle rail A barrier which prevents objects from falling from a shelf or stovetop because of the motion of a vessel.

fiddle block A block containing two sheaves, one above the other.

fife rail A rail around a mast which has holes to accept belaying pins.

fighting chair A stout seat which is firmly mounted to the sole of a cockpit as a support for an angler while reeling game fish in.

fin keel A deep, but short (fore to aft) keel.

fine (fīn) *adj.* Narrow or sharply pointed (*said of a bow or hull*).

fish finder An electronic instrument which uses sound waves to detect and locate fish beneath the boat.

fisherman sail A sail set between the masts of a schooner.

fix (fix) *n.* A confirmed navigational location of the boat.

fixed light A lighted aid to navigation with a steady (non-flashing) light.

flame arrestor A metal filter which covers the intake of a carburetor or fuel injection system to prevent flames from a backfire entering the engine compartment and igniting any fuel vapors which may be present.

flare (flār) *n.* 1. A pyrotechnic device which can be fired aloft to signal an emergency or provide illumination. 2. The outward curvature of a hull above the waterline.

flashing light A lighted aid to navigation whose "on" time is shorter than its "off" time. Compare OCCULTING LIGHT.

flatboat (flăt'bōt) *n.* 1. A flat-bottomed boat for use in shallow water. 2. A flat-bottomed boat whose weather deck is a flat platform for anglers to stand on. See Figure 14.

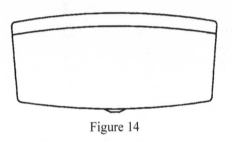

Figure 14

Flat Bottom Hull

flemish (flĕm'īsh) *v.* To lay a line in a flat spiral for storage on deck. Compare FAKE.

float (flōt) *n.* 1. A finger pier or raft. 2. An object that is designed to remain on the water's surface. -*v.* To remain on the surface of a liquid or aloft on a current of air.

float switch An electrical switch that is activated by a float; usually used to detect the presence of a rising liquid level. See BILGE PUMP.

flotation (flō-tā'shĕn) *n.* Air pockets or material such as foam included in a vessel's construction to increase its buoyancy.

flood tide The incoming or rising cycle of the tide.

flotsam (flôt'sĕm) *n.* Floating debris resulting from the destruction of a vessel. Compare JETSAM.

fluke (fl<u>oo</u>k) *n.* 1. The pointed part of an anchor. 2. A fin or blade-shaped projection.

flush deck A weather deck that is at the same level as the sheer.

flux gate compass See COMPASS.

flybridge *(also,* flying bridge) A control station situated above the main deck.

flying boat See SEAPLANE

foam core A layer of rigid foam laminated between two thin, durable outer layers to form a light, strong structural unit.

foghorn (fôg'hôrn) *n.* An audible aid to navigation, usually on-shore, activated during periods of reduced visibility.

folding propeller A propeller whose blades are pivoted to allow them to fold toward the shaft axis when not in use; used to reduce drag on a sailing vessel while not under power.

following sea Sea movement coming on a vessel's stern. Compare HEAD SEA.

forecastle (*also,* **fo'c's'le**) (fō'kë-sël) *n.* The forward space under the deck of a vessel, often the crew quarters.

foredeck (fôr'děk) *n.* The weather deck forward of the cabin or helm station.

foreguy A line used to control the position of a spinnaker pole on a topping lift.

forepeak (fôr'pēk) *n.* The deck area immediately above the bow.

forestay (fōr'stā) *n.* A stay running from high on the mast to the foredeck or bowsprit. 2. The innermost of multiple stays on a cutter. See HEADSTAY.

fore-triangle The space forward of the mast usually occupied by the foresail(s), bounded by the mast, forestay and deck.

forward (fôr'wërd) *adj.* At or near the bow. *-adv.* Toward the bow.

foul (foul) *adj.* 1. Having the potential to entangle. 2. Bad or undesirable (*as in foul weather*). *-v.* To entangle or interfere with.

founder (foun'dër) *v.* To sink.

fractional rig A sloop whose jib is hoisted from a position below the top of the mast. Compare MASTHEAD SLOOP.

frame (frām) *n.* 1. A supporting rib of a hull. 2. The skeletal hull structure comprised of individual frames and stringers. *-v.* To manufacture and erect the structural members prior to planking a hull.

freeboard (frē'bôrd) *n.* The part of the hull sides above the waterline; topsides.

fresh water cooling A plumbing arrangement that circulates raw (salt) water and the engine's cooling water through separate channels within a heat exchanger, cooling the engine while insulating it from the corrosive effects of raw water.

freshen (frĕsh 'ĕn) *v.* 1. To adjust lines or gear to prevent chafe. 2. Increasing wind speed.

fuel injection The precisely controlled introduction of pressurized fuel directly into the combustion chamber of an internal combustion engine. Less effective variations include injection into the intake airstream (throttle body injection) or at the cylinder's intake port (port injection).

furl (fûrl) *v.* To stow or remove from use by rolling up.

furlong (fŭr'lông) *n.* A unit of linear measurement equal to 660 feet.

futtock (fŭt'tôk) (*Usually pl.*, **futtocks**) *n.* One of the curved sections that are assembled to make up a rib in a hull frame.

G

gaff (găf) *n.* 1. A spar. 2. A long-handled hook used to land fish or capture distant objects.

gaff rigged Describing a fore-and-aft sail suspended from a spar in order to extend its top edge.

gain (gān) *n.* The directional efficiency of an antenna, especially in the ability to focus a transmitted signal in the horizontal axis.

galley (găl'ē) *n.* 1. The area of a vessel where food is prepared; the kitchen. 2. A shallow medieval vessel powered by sail and oars.

gallows frame A raised athwartships structure to support a boom. See BOOM CRUTCH.

gangplank (*also,* **gangway**) (găng'plănk, găng'wā) *n.* A temporary walkway from a vessel to a dock.

garboard (gär'bôrd) *n.* The plank or strake closest to the keel of a wooden vessel.

gear (gēr) *n.* Equipment, tools and apparel specific to the use of a boat.

gel coat The hard, brittle outer surface of a molded fiberglass structure, such as a hull, which provides a protective barrier and coloration.

generator (jĕn'ĕ-rā'tĕr) *n.* 1. A gasoline- or diesel-engine-powered system for producing AC electric power on board a vessel (*also* called a genset). 2. A belt-driven source of battery-charging (DC) power in older automotive and marine engine systems.

genny See GENOA.

genoa (jĕ'nō-ĕ) *n.* A large headsail that extends aft of the mast (*also called a* lapper).

genoa track A fore and aft track on which sheet blocks are adjusted and fastened.

genset See GENERATOR.

geographic coordinates Imaginary lines of latitude (North-to-South) and longitude (East-to-West) that encircle the earth to provide a commonly understood way to describe geographical position.

get-home An auxiliary means of propulsion to be used in the event of a failure in the main system.

gig (gīg) *n.* (*archaic*) A longboat reserved for a ship's officers.

gilguy (gīl'gī) *n* . A line to hold halyards away from mast to prevent the noise of them slapping in the wind.

gimbal (gīm'bĕl) *n.* 1. A mounting which pivots on one or more axes to allow a fixture (*such as a lamp or stove*) to remain in an upright position regardless of the vessel's motion. 2. A universal joint in the power train of an outdrive unit.

gin pole A small crane used to hoist heavy objects (*such as lobster traps*) aboard.

give-way Describing the vessel which does not have the right of way in an overtaking or crossing maneuver involving another vessel. Compare STAND-ON.

global positioning system (GPS) A navigation system which calculates and displays a precise determination of a receiver's geographical location using signals from a constellation of orbiting satellites. See DIFFERENTIAL GPS.

GMT See GREENWICH MEAN TIME

gooseneck (goos'nĕk) *n.* A universal joint for mounting a boom to a mast.

GPS See GLOBAL POSITIONING SYSTEM.

grapnell (grăp'nĕl) *n.* A small anchor-like device with several hooks arranged in a circular pattern, usually used for retrieval of overboard objects.

Greenwich Mean Time (*also*, Universal Time) The time at the Greenwich Meridian used for determining longitude and standard time in celestial navigation.

Greenwich Meridian (*also*, **Prime Meridian**) The line of longitude (zero degrees) that passes through Greenwich, England. See GREENWICH MEAN TIME.

grid (grīd) *n.* A matrix formed by lines intersecting at right angles on a chart.

groin (groin) *n.* A rigid linear structure built at right angles to the shore to reduce erosion.

grommet (grōm'ĕt) *n.* A metal or plastic ring inserted into a hole as a reinforcement or to protect lines or wires from chafing as they pass through it.

ground (ground) *n.* 1. The common side of an electrical circuit. 2. The side of an electrical circuit connected to the chassis or frame of a structure. 3. The negative side of most circuits. 4. The sea bottom.

ground plate A highly conductive metal plate mounted on the hull to ensure good contact between the vessel's electrical system and the water.

ground tackle The complete anchoring system, including anchor, chain, rode and any buoys or trip lines.

gudgeon (gŭd'j ĕn) *n.* A transom-mounted eye which accepts a pintle (pin) to form a pivot point for the rudder. See Figure 15.

gunkhole (gŭnk'hōl) *n.* A sheltered, out-of-the-way cove or inlet. -*v* To travel to such places.

gunwale (gŭn'ĕl) *n.* The upper edge of the side of the hull.

guy (gī) *n.* A line, sheet or cable being used as an active component of rigging. -v To attach, hold, or support an object with such a device.

gybe See JIBE.

gypsy (jīp'sē) *n.* A windlass spool or section of a spool which is shaped and indented to grip chain.

gyre (jīr) *n.* A very large circular ocean current.

gyroscope (jī'rō-skōp') *n.* A navigational device whose basis is a spinning mass such as a wheel which is mounted in a low-friction gimbal. The inertia of the spinning mass keeps the device in position regardless of the change in attitude of its surroundings.

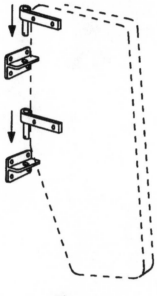

Figure 15

Gudgeons & Pintles

H

hail (hāl) *v.* To call to a party ashore or another vessel.

hailer (hāl'ër) *n.* An electronic microphone, amplifier and loudspeaker system for audibly broadcasting commands or communication.

halon (hā'lôn) *n.* A gas used in fire extinguishers.

halyard (hăl'y-rd) *n.* A line used to raise or lower sails, flags or spars.

hanging locker A tall closet for storing garments.

hank (hânk) *n.* A hook, shackle or other device for attaching a sail to a stay.

hardtop (härd'tôp) *n.* A rigid roof over a helm station or cockpit.

harness (här'nĕs) *n.* 1. An arrangement of lines or webbing used to distribute stress or loads. See BRIDLE. 2. A set of straps and buckles worn around the body and fitted with a secure attachment point. See SAFETY HARNESS.

hatch (hătch) *n.* An opening in a deck, hull or cabin with a hinged or removable cover, door or light.

haul (hôl) *v.* 1. To pull or tow. 2. To remove a vessel from the water.

hawse pipe An opening through which an anchor rode or other line is led.

hawser (hô'zër) *n.* A large-diameter line used for towing or tying up large vessels.

head (hĕd) *n.* 1. A marine toilet. 2. The top of a sail. *-v.* To move in a specific direction.

head off (*also* **bear off, fall off, pay off**) Turn away from the wind or a course.

head sea Sea movement coming on a vessel's bow. Compare FOLLOWING SEA.

heading (hĕd'ĭng) *n.* The direction of travel. See BEARING, AZIMUTH.

heading up Changing course to sail closer to the wind. Compare FALLING OFF.

headliner (hĕd'lĭn'ër) *n.* A fabric or cushioned covering applied to a deckhead.

headstay (hĕd'stā) *n.* The foremost of multiple forestays on a cutter. See FORESTAY.

heat exchanger 1. A device containing two independent, but thermally connected channels for the passage of liquids or air which enter at different temperatures and exit nearer equilibrium. 2. A radiator. 3. An intercooler.

heave to To bring or come to a stop.

heaving line See MESSENGER.

heel (hēl) (*often, to* heel *over*) *v.* To roll to the side; to list.

helm (hĕlm) *n.* 1. The wheel or tiller which steers a vessel. 2. The control station. 3. The responsibility for a vessel (*at* or *taking* the helm).

hermaphrodite brig A two-masted vessel with a square-rigged foremast and a fore-and-aft-rigged mainmast.

HID See HULL IDENTIFICATION NUMBER.

hike out To lean out over the gunwale to counterbalance heeling under sail. See TRAPEZE.

hiking strap A toe hold or rail to support crew while hiking out. See TRAPEZE.

hitch (hītch) *n.* 1. A knot (*especially a temporary attachment*). 2. An attachment point for a trailer. *-v.* To attach.

hogged (hôgd) *adv.* Condition of a hull where the bow and stern have drooped relative to mid-ships. Compare SAGGED.

hold (hōld) *n.* The area below a ship's deck for carrying cargo.

holding ground Term for the sea bottom when assessing its ability to hold an anchor.

holding tank An onboard tank for the storage of sewerage until it can be pumped out at a shore facility.

horn (hôrn) *n.* A device which produces an audible tone as a warning or signal.

horn cleat See CLEAT.

hot molded Bonded, laminated or impregnated with polyester or epoxy resins which require added heat to cure.

hound (hound) *n.* Attachment point on a mast where lower shrouds are secured.

houseboat (hous'bōt) *n.* A vessel whose main purpose is to provide living accommodations.

hull (hŭl) *n.* The main, buoyant part of a vessel.

hull identification number A distinctive number affixed to each new vessel by its manufacturer, showing the vessel's type, serial number, date of manufacture and manufacturer's identification.

hull speed Maximum displacement speed for a given hull before it attempts to go on plane. (*Theoretically equivalent to the square root of the waterline length multiplied by 1.34*)

hydrofoil (hī'drō-foil') *n.* 1. A wing-like device that is designed to plane in the water. 2. A vessel which rides on such devices.

hydroplane (hī'drō-plān') *n.* A high-powered speedboat designed to ride with minimum hull surface in contact with the water. *-v.* To move over the water in such a fashion.

I

I/O See INBOARD/OUTBOARD.

ICW See INTRACOASTAL WATERWAY.

impeller (im-pĕl'ĕr) *n.* 1. The rotor of a centrifugal or axial-flow pump or blower. 2. A paddlewheel used to detect and measure the flow of a liquid.

in irons Sailing directly into the wind.

inboard (īn'bôrd) *adj.* Located within the hull. *-adv.* Within the hull. *-n.* 1. An engine so located. 2. A vessel with engine(s) so located. See Figure 16.

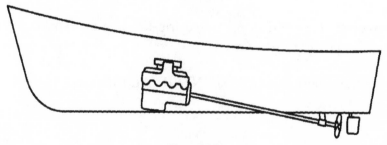

Figure 16

Inboard

inboard/outboard An arrangement where the power from an aft-mounted engine is directly transmitted through the transom to an articulated outdrive unit to which the propeller is mounted.

inflatable (ĭn'-flā'tĕ-bĕl) *n.* A boat constructed of flexible material formed into sealed chambers into which air is pumped to provide buoyancy.

inland navigation rules (The 1980 U.S. Inland Navigation Rules) Rules of the nautical road which apply to vessels operating in harbors, as well as certain rivers, lakes and inland waterways. Compare COLREGS.

inland waterway Any navigable waterway within the geographical boundaries of a continent.

intercooler (ĭn'tĕr-kool'ĕr) *n.* A heat exchanger inserted between a turbo-charger or super-charger and the engine to cool the incoming air or air/fuel mixture to increase its density.

intracoastal waterway (ICW) A system of interconnected bays and canals along the Atlantic and Gulf coasts which allow vessels to travel in protected waters.

inverter (ĭn-vûr'tĕr) *n.* An electrical device that converts DC power to AC power.

isophase light See EQUAL INTERVAL LIGHT.

J

jackline (jăk'līn) *n.* A line to which a safety harness is attached.

jackshaft (jăk'shăft) *n.* A drive shaft connecting a mid-ships-mounted engine to an outdrive unit at the stern. See Figure 17.

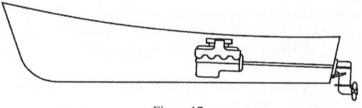

Figure 17

Jackshaft

jacob's ladder A rope ladder with rigid rungs.

jenny See GENOA.

jet boat A boat which is propelled by the force of a stream of water expelled from an aft orifice.

jetsam (jĕt'sĕm) *n.* Floating material that has been jettisoned from a vessel. Compare FLOTSAM.

jettison (jĕt'ĕ-sĕn) *v.* To cast cargo overboard to lighten the vessel. See JETSAM.

jetty (jĕt'ē) *n.* 1. A protective seawall built out into the water. 2. A pier built at right angles to the shoreline.

jib (jīb) *n.* A triangular foresail.

jibboom (jīb'boom) *n.* An extension of a bowsprit.

jibe (jīb) *v.* To shift a fore-and-aft sail from one side of a vessel to the other while sailing before the wind.

jiffy reef A series of ties built into a sail which allow its lower edge to be gathered in order to shorten the sail.

jigger (jīg'ĕr) *n.* Mizzen mast or sail of a ketch or yawl.

jonboat jôn'bōt (also, johnboat) *n.* A small utility craft with a flat bottom and a square prow; often made of aluminum and used to navigate shallow water.

joinery (join'ĕr-ē) *n.* The woodwork, cabinetry and trim in a vessel's cabin or salon.

jumper stays Intermediate stays attached to the mast at mid-height.

junk (jŭnk) *n.* Chinese vessel with battened sails and a high poopdeck.

K

kedge (kĕdj) *n.* A light anchor used in warping a vessel. *-v.* To warp a vessel by means of a kedge.

keel (kēl) *n.* 1. The lowest fore-and-aft structural member of a hull. 2. The central fore-and-aft ridge of a molded hull. 3. A blade-shaped projection below the keel to counteract heeling under sail (*also called a* ballast keel).

keelboat (kēl'bōt) *n.* A shallow-draft river freighter with a keel.

keelhaul (kēl'hôl) (*archaic*) *v.* To tow a person in the water from one side of a vessel down under the keel and up the other as a form of punishment.

keelson (kēl'sën) *n.* A longitudinal structural member above the frames, parallel and connected to the keel.

ketch (kĕtch) *n.* A two-masted, fore-and-aft-rigged sailing vessel with a shorter mizzen mast set aft of the main mast but forward of the rudder post. Compare YAWL.

kill switch An emergency switch which shuts off ignition power to stop the engine.

king plank The center board of a wooded laid deck.

knee (nē) *n.* An "L-shaped" member which is fastened to the top of a hull frame to connect and support a deck beam. See TAMARACK.

knightshead (nīts'hĕd) *n.* A timber which rises from the keel of a sailing vessel to support the aft end of the bowsprit.

knockabout (nôk'ĕ-bout') *n.* A small sloop with a mainsail, jib and keel, but without a bowsprit.

knot[(1)] (nôt) *n.* A fastening device made by tying the ends or sections of cordage together in a prescribed way.

knot[(2)] (nôt) *n.* A nautical mile (*used when referring to speed or velocity made good*).

L

lacing (lā'sīng) *n.* Line used to secure a sail to a spar.

landmark (lănd'märk) *n.* Any point of reference on shore.

lanyard (lăn'yērd) *n.* A small-diameter line that is used as a trip wire or safety device.

lapper (lăp'ēr) *n.* A foresail that extends aft of the mast.

lapstrake (lăp'strāk) *n.* 1. A hull plank which overlaps the one below it. 2. A hull or vessel so constructed. *-adj.* Constructed with overlapping planks.

larboard (lär'bērd) (*archaic*) *n.* Port. *-adj.* On the port side.

large navigational buoy (LNB) A very large, deep-water aid to navigation, often including automated weather monitoring devices which broadcast reports to a central location.

lash (lăsh) *v.* To tie down securely.

lateen (lä-tēn') *adj.* Describing a sail or rigging where a triangular sail is suspended from a long yard at an angle to a short mast. *-n.* A vessel so rigged.

latitude (l ăt'ë-t<u>oo</u>d) *n.* The distance north or south from the Equator; measured in degrees, minutes and seconds and marked on charts with lines called Parallels.

launch (lônch) *n.* A small, open boat used to ferry passengers. -*v.* 1. To place a vessel into the water. 2. To commission a vessel.

lay (lā) *n.* The direction of a rope's twist.

lazarette (lăz'ë-rĕt') *n.* A storage locker at or near the stern.

lazyjack (lā'zē-jăk') *n.* A line from the mast to the boom that catches the sail when it's lowered.

lead line (pronounced *led* line) A line which is weighted and marked at intervals for use in determining water depth.

led (lĕd) *adv.* Brought to or through a block, guide or opening. (*Said of lines or sheets*)

lee (lē) *n.* 1. The side away from the direction from which the wind is blowing. 2. Shelter from the wind. -*adj.* Sheltered from the wind. -*adv.* (*often*, alee) Toward shelter.

lee tide A tide running ahead of the wind. Compare WEATHER TIDE.

leech (lēch) *n.* The trailing edge of a sail.

leeward (lē'wërd, l<u>oo</u>'-rd) *adj.* Toward the lee.

leeway (lē'wā) *n.* Sideways drift of a vessel while under way, usually caused by wind or current on the beam.

length overall The total length of a vessel, from stem to stern, not including accessories such as bow pulpits or swim platforms.

life buoy A throwable ring- or "U"-shaped flotation device.

lifeline (līf'līn) *n.* A line around the deck to keep persons from falling overboard.

light list A Coast Guard publication which lists the location and characteristics of aids to navigation in the region for which it's published.

limber hole A drain hole through frames or stringers which allows water to flow into the bilge.

line (līn) *n.* Any rope or cable used aboard or attached to a vessel.

line of position (LOP) In navigation, an imaginary line along which the a vessel can be presumed to be located.

linestopper (*also* **lineclutch**) A fitting through which a line is led, having cam-action pinchers to keep tension on the line.

list (līst) *v.* To lean to one side. *-n.* The attitude of a vessel that has leaned over.

live ballast Any mass, such as water in a tank, which can be added, removed or shifted to adapt to changing conditions a vessel may encounter.

livewell (līv'wĕl) *n.* A baitwell provided with circulating water to keep bait alive in storage.

LNB See LARGE NAVIGATIONAL BUOY.

LNM See LOCAL NOTICE TO MARINERS.

LOA See LENGTH OVERALL.

load water line (LWL) The length of a normally loaded hull at the water line.

lobster yacht A vessel based on a traditional lobster boat hull, but with a larger cabin and cruising accommodations provided.

local attraction Localized magnetic interference, not on the vessel, which may cause the vessel's compass to display inaccurate readings.

local notice to mariners A weekly Coast Guard publication and broadcast which lists new or uncharted hazards, conditions, temporary or permanent changes to charted aids to navigation and activities which may impact navigation in the area for which it's published.

lock (lôk) *n.* A chamber with opening gates at either end whose water level can be raised or lowered to transport vessels between different water levels on a canal or river.

locker (lôk'ër) *n.* A storage compartment.

loft (lôft) *v.* To transfer shapes from one scale to another, as from drawings to a full-size rendering or pattern.

log (lôg) *n.* (Also **Ship's Log**) A record of a vessel's use, travels and maintenance.

longboat (lông'bōt) *n.* A long, narrow boat with multiple rowing stations, often used as a lifeboat.

longitude (lôn'jë-tood') *n.* The distance east and west from the

Prime (Greenwich) Meridian to the International Date Line, measured in degrees, minutes and seconds and shown on charts as lines called Meridians.

loom (lo͞om) *n.* The glow of a light source that is below the horizon or obscured by fog.

LOP See LINE OF POSITION.

LORAN (lô-răn') *n.* A LOng RAnge Navigation system which calculates position by comparing time differences (TDs) between radio signals from two on-shore transmitters.

loud-hailer See HAILER.

lower shrouds Shrouds which attach to the mast below the spreader. Compare UPPER SHROUDS.

lower unit The part of an outdrive unit which contains the propeller shaft and its drive gear.

lubber's line An index line on a compass which, when aligned with a point on the card or dome, indicates the vessel's bearing.

luff (lŭf) *n.* 1. The act of sailing into the wind. 2. The forward part of a fore-and-aft sail. 3. The vertical measurement of a sail. *-v.* 1. To steer into the wind, especially with sails flapping. 2. To flap while losing wind (*said of a sail*).

lug sail A four-sided sail lacking a boom and bent to a yard which is attached to the mast at a slant.

lunch hook (*informal*) A light anchor.

LWL See LOAD WATER LINE

M

macerator (măs'ë-rā'tër) *n.* A pump which reduces solids to smaller particles as it pumps sewage into or from a holding tank.

magnetic North North as indicated by the reading of a magnetic compass, which varies from true (geographical) North by a factor which depends on the location of the vessel.

mainmast (mān'măst) *n.* The principal or tallest mast of a multi-masted vessel.

mainsail (mān'sāl; mān'sēl) *n.* The largest or principal sail on a mast.

mainsheet (mān'shēt) *n.* The line or tackle which controls the position of the mainsail boom.

marconi rig Triangular sail(s) set above a schooner's mainsail (s).

marina (mär-ē'nä) *n.* A shore-side facility for launching and berthing boats.

marine railroad (Also **railway**) A set of ways at the water's edge on which vessels can be launched or hauled.

marine sanitation device (MSD) An onboard toilet connected to a holding tank.

marine (mär-ē'n) *adj.* On, in or having to do with the sea or navigation thereon.

marlin tower See TUNA TOWER.

marlinspike (mär'lĭn-spīk') *n.* A smooth, pointed shaft used as a tool in splicing lines *(also called a* fid).

marlinspike seamanship Skills in working with lines, splices and knots.

martingale (mär'tĭn-gāl') *n.* A strut which runs forward and down from the stem to a point on a bobstay. *(also called a* dolphin striker) See Figure 18.

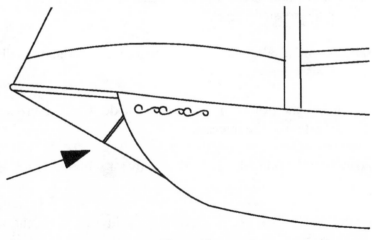

Figure 18

Martingale or Dolphin Striker

masthead (măst'hĕd) *n.* The top of a mast.

masthead sloop A sloop whose jib is hoisted from the top of the mast. Compare FRACTIONAL RIG.

Mayday (mā'dā) *n.* A first-priority signal word used to indicate that a radio broadcast concerns a vessel in distress with the imminent danger of loss of life or the vessel. See PAN-PAN and SECURITÉ.

mean high water The average level of high tide in a given geographical area.

mean low water The average level of low tide in a given geographical area.

meeting vessel A vessel on a course that will result in a collision with another if no action is taken.

mercator projection A chart representation where the meridians of longitude and parallels of latitude are shown at right angles to each other, resulting in the apparent enlargement of areas as their distance from the equator increases.

meridian (mĕ-rīd'ē-ĕn) *n.* A line of longitude, part of a great circle which intersects both poles.

messenger (mĕs'sĕn-jĕr) *n.* A light line which is thrown and used to haul a heavier one (*also called a* heaving line).

MHW See MEAN HIGH WATER.

mizzen (mīz'ĕn) *n.* 1. A fore-and-aft sail set on a mizzenmast. 2. A short, secondary mast.

mizzenmast (mīz'ĕn-măst') *n.* 1. The aft mast of a ketch or yawl. 2. The third mast aft on a vessel with three or more masts. 3. A short, secondary mast. 4. A jigger mast.

MLW See MEAN LOW WATER.

modified deep V Generally, a hull with a deadrise angle of less than 20 degrees at the stern. See Figure 19.

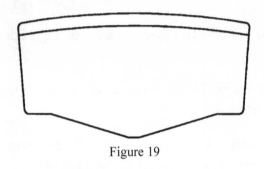

Figure 19

Modified V Planning Hull (16°)

mold (mōld) *n.* A tool into or onto which material can be formed to produce an object that is a mirror image of the mold. *-v.* To produce an object with the use of such a tool.

mold schedule The list of material layers and their order as used in laying up a structure in a mold.

monkey fist (*also,* **monkey's fist**) A complex knot that is formed around a weight at the end of a light line to enhance its ability to be thrown.

monohull (môn'ō-hŭl') *n.* A vessel with a single hull. Compare CATAMARAN, TRIMARAN.

moor (moor) *-v.* To secure a vessel by lines or chains.

mooring (moor'ĭng) *n.* 1. A semi-permanent anchor or weight with a rode connected to a pennant on a float, to which a vessel may be tied up. 2. The act of tying up to such a device. 3. An anchorage.

motor sailer A vessel which is designed to perform equally under sail or power.

motor yacht A large power boat with luxurious accommodations aboard.

mouse (mous) *v.* To wrap a line or small stuff across the mouth of a hook to prevent it from losing its purchase.

MSD See MARINE SANITATION DEVICE.

multihull (mŭl'tĭ-hŭl') *n.* A vessel with more than one hull. See CATAMARAN, TRIMARAN.

mushroom anchor An anchor comprised of a heavy dish with a shank set into the center of it's concave side; often used as a mooring.

N

nameboard (nām'bôrd) *n.* A plaque mounted on a vessel with the vessel's name painted or engraved on it.

nautical (nô'tī-kĕl') *adj.* Pertaining to boats, boaters or navigation.

nautical mile A unit of linear measure equal to 6080 feet. (*called a knot only when used in describing speed*).

nav station An area, usually below, having a chart table and navigation tools and instruments.

naval architect A designer of marine vessels.

navigate (năv'ĕ-gāt') *v.* To plan and control the course of a vessel.

navigation lights White or colored lights which must be shown in prescribed patterns and locations on a vessel operating at night or under conditions of reduced visibility.

navigation (năv'ĕ-gā'shĕn) *n.* The theory and practice of guiding a vessel to a destination over a planned course.

navigator's balls See QUADRANTAL CORRECTORS.

neap tide A tide of the lowest range, occurring when the sun and moon are in quadrature (*also called a* drain tide).

NM See NAUTICAL MILE.

NMEA 0183 A standard for digital information exchange between navigation and communication devices promulgated by the National Marine Electronics Association.

non-skid A rough surface or serrated pattern applied or molded into steps, walkways or decking to provide secure footing.

normanpin (nōr'mën'pīn) *n.* A horizontal pin in a bitt or samson post to keep a line from coming free. See Figure 20.

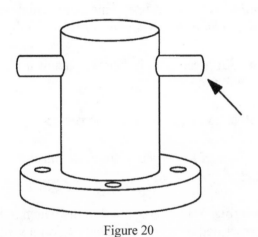

Figure 20

Normanpin

nun (nŭn) *n.* A red, even-numbered, floating aid to navigation in the shape of a cylinder which is tapered toward the top.

O

oakum (ō'kŭm) *n.* Hemp or jute fiber used in caulking the seams of wooden vessels.

oar (ōr) *n.* A long, thin pole with a blade at one end used to propel or sometimes steer a boat.

oarlock (ōr'lôk) *n.* A removable yoke which is set into the gunwale and used as a pivot for an oar.

occulting light A lighted aid to navigation whose "on" time is longer than its "off" time. Compare FLASHING LIGHT.

oilskins (oil'skīnz) *n.* Older term for foul-weather clothing.

on the hump (*informal*) The bow-up attitude of a vessel during the transition from displacement speed to planing.

outboard (out'bôrd) *adv.* Toward the outside of a vessel. *-adj.* Positioned outside a vessel. *-n.* 1. A motor attached to a vessel's transom or a bracket aft of the transom. 2. A boat so equipped. See Figure 21.

outdrive See STERN DRIVE.

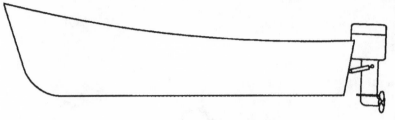

Figure 21

Outboard

outrigger (out'rĭg-ĕr) *n.* 1. A stabilizing secondary hull or pontoon set out to the side and attached to the main hull by struts. 2. A pivoting boom through which a fishing line is led to position the bait outside of the vessel's wake while under way.

overhead (ō'v-r-hĕd') *n.* The deckhead of a cabin or space below deck. (*What would be called a ceiling ashore.*)

P

packet (păk'ĕt) *n.* A vessel which plies a specific route carrying passengers and freight.

packing gland A mechanical sealing device which compresses a malleable material around a shaft to form an active seal. See STUFFING BOX.

paddle (păd'ĕl) *n.* A short oar which is used without an oarlock to propel or steer a small boat or canoe.

painter (pān'tĕr) *n.* (often used interchangeably with **pennant**) 1. A short mooring line. 2. Any short extension line.

Pan-Pan (*pronounced* pähn-pähn) A second-priority signal phrase used to indicate that a radio broadcast contains urgent information concerning the safety of a vessel or person. See MAYDAY and SECURITÉ.

parallel rulers A navigational tool used to offset courses on a chart; comprised of two rulers connected by a mechanism which allows them to be spread apart while remaining parallel to each other.

pay off (*also,* **bear off, head off, fall off**) To steer away from the wind.

pay out   To deploy a line or rode in a controlled manner. Compare RUN.

pedestal   (pĕd'ĕs-tĕl)   *n.* A mounting post for a binnacle, often supporting a wheel as well.

pelican hook   A hinged hook held closed by a ring or latch across its mouth.

pennant   See PAINTER.

personal flotation device   **(PFD)**   A vest or jacket containing flotation material to provide the wearer with additional buoyancy in the water; a life jacket.

PFD   See PERSONAL FLOTATION DEVICE.

picnic boat   See DAY BOAT.

pier   (pîr)   *n.* A dock structure set at right angles to the shore. Compare WHARF.

pile   (*also*, **piling**) (pīl, pīl'ĭng)   *n.* A pole driven into the seabed for use as a marker, to tie up a vessel or support a pier or other structure.

pilot house   An enclosed area for a helm station.

pilot house motor yacht   A yacht with an enclosed helm station forward.

pinch   (pīnch)   *v.* To sail so close to the wind as to stall.

pinky   (pīnk'ē)   *n.* A double-ended, eighteenth-century fishing schooner with a bluff bow and upswept bulwarks aft which led to a high triangular transom.

pinnace (pĭn'ĭ s) *n.* A small sailing tender.

pintle (pĭn'tĕl) *n.* A pin with a bracket that allows it to be mounted to a rudder, forming a pivot when inserted into a gudgeon on the transom.

pirogue (pĭ r'ōg) *n.* A canoe-shaped boat.

pitch (pĭtch) *n.* The theoretical distance a propeller will travel through the water on a single rotation. *-v.* To rock on a fore-and-aft axis.

pitchpole (pĭtch'pōl) v. To roll forward, stern over bow. See TRIP.

plane (plān) *v.* To use hydrodynamic lift to travel on top of the water (*rather than through it*).

planing hull A hull which, by its design, will rise up and travel on top of the water at speed. Compare DISPLACEMENT HULL.

plank (*also,* **planking**) (plănk, plănk'ĭng) *n.* The longitudal outer member(s) of a wooden hull (*also called a* strake).

plot (plŏt) *n.* The graphical representation of information such as a course or a chart. *-v.* To create such information.

plumb bow A bow with a vertical stem.

point (point) *n.* 1. One of the 32 named compass headings, 11.25 degrees apart. 2. The ability to sail close to the wind. *-v* To sail close to the wind. See Table 2.

POINTS OF THE COMPASS

Point	Degrees	Minutes
North	0	0
North by East	11	15
North Northeast	22	30
Northeast by North	33	45
Northeast	45	0
Northeast by East	56	15
East Northeast	67	30
East by North	78	45
East	90	0
East by South	101	15
East Southeast	112	30
Southeast by East	123	45
Southeast	135	0
Southeast by South	146	15
South Southeast	157	30
South by East	168	45
South	180	0
South by West	191	15
South Southwest	202	30
Southwest by South	213	45
Southwest	225	0
Southwest by West	236	15
West Southwest	247	30
West by South	258	45
West	270	0
West by North	281	15
West Northwest	292	30
Northwest by West	303	45
Northwest	315	0
Northwest by North	326	15
North Northwest	337	30
North by West	348	45
North	0	0

Table 2

points of sailing The angles relative to the wind on which a vessel can sail. See Figure 22.

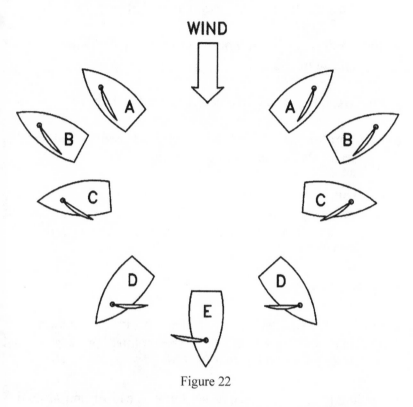

Figure 22

Points of Sailing. A) Close-Hauled, B) Close Reach,
C) Beam Reach, D) Broad Reach, E) Run

pole (pōl) *v.* To propel a boat in shallow water by pushing against the sea bottom with a pole.

pontoon boat A vessel which rides on two or more pontoons (*also called a* deck boat).

poop (*also,* **poopdeck**) (poop, poop-děk') *n.* A raised stern deck.

port (pôrt) *n.* 1. A harbor or other refuge for boats. 2. The left side of a vessel when viewed from the stern. *-adv.* Toward the left side. *-adj.* On the left side.

pram (prăm) *n.* A flat-bottomed rowboat with squared bow and stern.

Prime Meridian See GREENWICH MERIDIAN.

proa (prō'ë) *n.* A fast Malayan boat with a gaff-rigged triangular sail and a single outrigger.

prop walk The paddlewheel effect of a rotating propeller, resulting in the tendency of a single-screw vessel to drift to the side, especially in reverse. See COUNTER-ROTATING.

prop See PROPELLER.

propeller (prō'-pĕl'ër) *n.* A device with two or more angled blades set on a hub, which when rotated, propels a vessel through the water. See PITCH.

propeller cage A protective structure ahead of and around a propeller to keep it from being fouled.

propeller pocket A recess which allows the propeller to be mounted higher in the hull, reducing the vessel's draft.

propeller shaft The round, solid metal bar which transmits power from the marine gear to the propeller. Compare JACKSHAFT.

protractor (prō'trăk'tër) *n.* 1. A device consisting of an arm which rotates on a (semi)circular scale which is indexed in degrees; used in determining the angular relationship between two lines or objects. 2. A printed representation of the scale such as a compass rose.

prow (prôw) *n.* The bow of a vessel.

PT boat A light, fast torpedo-launching boat. (*Patrol Torpedo*)

pulpit (pŭl'pīt) *n.* A raised platform. See BOW PULPIT.

pump-out 1. The act of removing sewage from a vessel's holding tank. 2. The station at which it's accomplished.

punt (pŭnt) *n.* A small, flat-bottomed boat, usually propelled by poling.

purchase (pûr'chĕs) *n.* An advantageous grip, hold or attachment to an object in preparation for using or moving it.

Q

quadrantal correctors (*also,* **quadrantal spheres** or **navigators' balls**) Iron masses mounted on a binnicle to compensate for compass deviations caused by onboard conditions.

quadrantal spheres See QUADRANTAL CORRECTORS.

quarter (kwôr'tër) *n.* The side of a vessel from amidships to the stern.

quarter berth A sleeping area on either side of a vessel under the helm or the cockpit.

quarterdeck (kwôr'tër-dĕk') *n.* The after part of the upper deck of a vessel.

quartering (kwôr'tër- īng') *adv.* Toward or from the quarter. -*adj.* On the quarter.

quay (kē, or kwā) *n.* A stone or concrete pier, usually parallel to the shoreline.

R

RADAR **(RAdio Detecting And Ranging)** A method of detecting and locating distant objects through the analysis of radio waves reflected from them.

radar arch An athwartships structure above the helm or cabin for mounting RADAR and other antennas.

radar reflector A metal device hung aloft on a vessel to enhance its visibility to others' RADAR detectors.

radio direction finder A receiver with a rotating antenna which determines the bearing of a distant transmitter (on a vessel) by the bearing of the antenna when the strength of radio signals being received from the vessel are strongest.

radio telephone A transceiver. See VHF.

raft (räft) *n*. A floating platform. -*v*. To tie up to another boat.

rail (rāl) *n*. A tubular structure supported by stanchions around the perimeter of a deck to help prevent crew from falling overboard.

rake (rāk) *n.* An aft-leaning angle of a mast relative to the deck.

range (rānj) *n.* A pair of landmarks or aids to navigation which, when lined up, will position the viewer on a line of position or in a channel.

range light A light which is one of a pair of markers used as an aid to navigation. See RANGE.

ratline (răt'l-n) *n.* Rope rung(s) strung between adjoining shrouds for use as a ladder.

raw water cooling A system which circulates raw (sea) water directly through the engine cooling system. Compare FRESH WATER COOLING.

raw water pump An engine-driven pump to circulate raw (sea) water through a heat exchanger.

reach (rēch) *n.* Any point of sailing between 45 and 180 degrees off the wind. *-v.* To sail with the wind abeam. See BEAM, BROAD , CLOSE .

reciprocal course A return course, 180 degrees from the present course.

reduction gear A transmission or speed-reducer used to match an engine's output to the requirements of the hull and its operation conditions.

reef[1] (rēf) *n.* A submerged rock or coral shoal.

reef[2] (rēf) *v.* To reduce the area of sail in use.

reeve (rēv) *v.* To lead a line through a block or fairlead.

regatta (rë-gä'të) *n.* A boat race.

relative bearing The direction of an object measured in relation to the bow, which is designated 000 degrees.

resin (rĕz'ĭn) *n.* 1. A viscous liquid epoxy or polyester compound used to bond, laminate or impregnate fiberglass and other materials in the manufacture of boats and components. See FRP and COLD MOLDING. 2. A component of varnish and shellac.

reverse transom A transom which slants forward from bottom to top.

rhumb line A course which crosses all meridians at the same angle.

rib (rĭb) *n.* A structural frame in a vessel's hull.

ribband (rĭb'bănd) *n.* A flexible strip used to hold ribs in place while hull planking is attached.

RIBI See RIGID BOTTOM INFLATABLE.

ride (rĭd) *v.* To lie at anchor.

riding sail A small sail set aft to keep an anchored vessel headed into the wind.

rig (rĭg) *n.* An arrangement or device. -*v.* To install, outfit or equip in a specific manner.

rigging (rĭg'ĭng) *n.* All of a sailboat's above-deck lines, sails, spars and their fittings.

rigging knife   A sharp, folding knife equipped with a marlinspike.

right (rīt)   *v.* To return to a normal position after capsizing or heeling excessively.

rigid bottom inflatable   An inflatable boat whose bottom is a molded pan with hull-like features.

rip current   See UNDERTOW.

rip tide   A tidal flow in a basin or river which results in broken water because of interaction with another current or by coursing over obstructions on the bottom.

riprap   (rīp'răp)   *n.* Large pieces or slabs of stone, often granite, used as a protective barrier at water's edge.

roach   (roach)   *n.* A convex curve at the leech of a sail.

roadsted   (rōd'stĕd)   *n.* A temporary anchorage for vessels waiting to tie up.

rocker   (rôk'ër)   *n.* The fore-to-aft curvature of a vessel's bottom.

rocket launcher   (*informal*)   Multiple cylindrical receptacles for fishing rods, mounted to an athwartships bracket or arch.

rode   (rōd)   *n.* The line, cable, chain and fittings for an anchor.

rodholder   (rōd'hōl'dër)   *n.* A cylindrical receptacle recessed into the gunwale or other surface to hold a fishing rod.

roller furling   A mechanical system which allows a sail to be furled around a rotating spar or stay.

roller reefing A mechanical system which allows the foot of a sail to be furled around a rotating spar or boom.

rowboat A small boat propelled by rowing with oars.

rub rail A protective protrusion, usually a rope or rubber molding, around the outermost extremity of a hull.

rub strake See RUB RAIL.

rudder (rŭd'dër) *n.* A pivoting blade suspended directly behind a propeller from or below the transom which can be turned from the helm to steer a vessel.

rudder post (Also **Rudder stock**) The vertical shaft on which a rudder pivots.

rule of twelfths A rule for estimating the amount of depth change that will occur during various stages of the tide.

RULE OF TWELFTHS

HOUR	1	2	3	4	5	6
CHANGE	1/12	2/12	3/12	3/12	2/12	1/12

run (rŭn) *v.* Let out in an uncontrolled manner. ("Let it run", *said of a line.*) Compare PAY OUT.

run before the wind To sail with the wind abaft.

runabout (rŭn'ë-bout') *n.* A small, open boat.

running light See NAVIGATION LIGHTS.

running rigging Halyards, sheets and other rigging that is set, adjusted or removed during the course of normal sailing maneuvers. Compare STANDING RIGGING.

S

SA See SELECTIVE AVAILABILITY

sacrificial anode A conductive mass, usually zinc, attached to metal equipment below the waterline of a boat. The zinc, being a less noble metal, is eroded by the effects of electrolysis, shielding the equipment from damage.

safety harness A body harness with a line and shackle that allow it to be attached to a lifeline; used to attach crew to the boat during rough weather or single-handing.

sagged (sâgd) *adv.* A condition of a hull where the mid-ship section has drooped relative to the bow and stern. Compare HOGGED.

sail (sāl) *n.* A vertical airfoil which uses wind to propel a vessel.

sail plan The compliment of sails for a given condition, rigging or vessel.

salon (*also* **saloon**) (sä-lōn', -loon') *n.* A lounge or living area within the cabin or below.

sampan (săm'păn) *n.* A flat-bottomed skiff used in the Orient.

samson post A very sturdy bitt in the bow or at the stern.

sand shoe A stout, metal bar connecting the skeg to the bottom of the rudder post, providing protection for the rudder and propeller in case of a grounding.

scantlings (skănt'līngs) *n.* The material and size specifications of a (wooden) hull's components.

scarf (skärf) *n.* A butt joint between similar pieces of material, where the ends are cut at an angle and overlapped to maintain the original thickness. In the case of a bonded joint, its strength is greatly improved by the increased bonding area.

schooner (skoo'nër) *n.* A ship with two or more fore-and-aft rigged masts, the mainmast being taller than the foremast.

scope (skōp) *n.* The ratio of the length of a rode or mooring line to the depth of the water. *(Ex: 180 ft long rode in 30ft of water = 6:1 scope)*

scow (skou) *n.* A large, flat-bottomed boat with square bow and stern, usually used for hauling freight.

screw (skroo) *n.* Propeller.

scull (skŭl) *n.* 1. A small, light racing boat. 2. A long oar used to propel a boat. -*v.* To propel a boat by moving an oar in a figure eight pattern in the water at its stern.

scupper (skŭp'ër) *n.* An opening in the bulwark or transom to allow water to drain from the deck or cockpit.

scuttle (skŭt'ĕl) *v.* To intentionally sink a vessel by opening through-hull fittings or holing the hull.

sea (sē) *n.* 1. A large body of (usually salt-) water. 2. Term used to refer to all of the conditions of a body of water which affect vessels and navigation.

sea anchor A device in the form of a parachute which is tied, usually to the bow of a vessel and dropped overboard at the end of a long line to arrest its forward motion, allowing it to safely ride out high winds and heavy seas.

sea keeping The behavior of a vessel at sea.

sea kindly Safe, stable and easy to handle at sea. *(Said of a boat)*

sea room A safe distance from shore or hazards; space to maneuver.

seacock (sē'kôk) *n.* A valve which controls the flow of water through a through-hull opening, such as a cooling water inlet.

seamanship (sē'm-n-shīp') *n.* Skill in managing the operation and piloting of a vessel.

seaplane (sē'plān) *n.* An airplane with pontoons or a hull shape which allow it to take off and land in water.

seaworthy (sē'wûr'thē) *adj.* Capable of being safely used at sea.

secure (sī-kyoor') *v.* 1. To make fast; belay. *(secure a line to a cleat)* 2. To protect from harm.

Securité (sī-kyoor'ë-tā') *n.* A third-priority signal word used to indicate that a radio broadcast contains a warning or information concerning navigation, safety or weather. See MAYDAY and PAN-PAN.

sedan cruiser A boat whose predominant feature is a large cabin on its main deck.

seiner (sān'ër) *n.* A commercial boat which fishes with a net suspended below the surface from floats. Compare DRAGGER.

seize (sēz) *v.* To bind the end of a line with small stuff to prevent unraveling.

selective availablilty The deliberate occasional degradation of the performance of the Global Positioning Satellite system by the Department of Defense to discourage unintended use.

self-steering A mechanical system, usually a windvane attached to the rudder post of a sailboat, used to keep a sailboat headed into the wind.

self-bailing Condition where the deck or cockpit sole of a vessel is far enough above the water line to ensure that water taken aboard will run out of the scuppers unaided.

self-righting Where a vessel's center of gravity, ballast and flotation are placed to cause it to return upright unaided after capsizing.

semi-displacement hull A cruising hull designed to run efficiently at displacement speeds while retaining the ability to operate on plane at higher speeds. See Figure 23.

sentinel (sĕn'tĕ-nĕl') *n.* A weight attached to a rode between the anchor and the vessel to keep the anchor chain horizontal to maximize holding power.

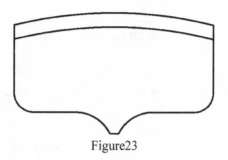

Figure23

Semi-Displacement (Soft Chine)

set (sĕt) *v.* Hoist or deploy (*a sail or other gear*).

sextant (sĕx'tĕnt) *n.* A navigational instrument for measuring the altitude of heavenly bodies.

shackle (shăk'ĕl) *n.* A "U"-Shaped metal bracket with a removable pin or bolt across its open end. -*v.* To fasten with the aid of a shackle. See Figure 24.

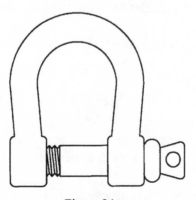

Figure 24

Shackle

shaft log See STUFFING BOX.

shallop (shăl'ĕp) *n.* A small, open boat that can be rowed or sailed.

shank (shânk) *n.* The main member of an anchor between the arm and the eye.

sharpie (shär'pē) *n.* A narrow, flat-bottomed New England fishing vessel with a centerboard and triangular sail(s) on its mast(s).

shear pin A pin which locates a propeller or other device on a shaft, designed to protect the propeller by failing in the event of being overburdened.

sheave (shīv) *n.* The rotating grooved wheel in a block. A pulley wheel.

sheer (*also*, **shear**) (shēr) *n.* The upward curve or degree of curvature of the upper edge of a hull as viewed from the side.
sheer clamp A longitudal support at the intersection of the deck and topsides or along the gunwales.

sheet (shēt) *n.* A line attached to one or both lower corners of a sail.

sheet block A block for sheet tackle or one that leads a sheet to a winch.

shell (shĕl) *n.* 1. The outer case of a block. 2. A racing scull.

ship (shĭp) *n.* A waterborne vessel, usually over 65 feet (20m) in length. See BOAT. *-v.* To involuntarily take something aboard, (*such as water in rough seas*).

shoal (shoal) *n.* A shallow area in otherwise navigable water. -*v.* To become shallow.

shoal draft Having minimized hull depth below the water line, so able to navigate in shallow water.

shore power 110 or 220 volt AC electricity connected to a vessel while docked.

short stay An anchor rode with reduced or insufficient scope.

shorten sail To reef a sail.

shroud (shroud) *n.* A structural line or cable stretched from the top of a mast to chainplates in the topsides or deck of a sailboat; part of the standing rigging.

sidelight See NAVIGATION LIGHT

single side band (SSB) A type of short-wave radio transmission used for long-distance communication.

single up Reduce docklines to one point in preparation for casting off.

skeg (skĕg) *n.* 1. An extension of the keel brought down and aft to the bottom of a rudder post to protect the rudder and the propeller. 2. A blade extending downward from an outboard motor or the lower unit of a stern drive to enhance steering effectiveness. See Figure 25.

skiff (skīf) *n.* A flat-bottomed, shallow-draft rowboat having a pointed bow and square stern.

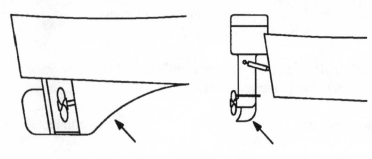

Figure 25

Skegs

skipjack (skīp'jăk') *n.* 1. An evolved fishing boat design of the Chesapeake Bay area. 2. A food fish resembling and related to the tuna.

slack (slăk) *n.* The lack of tension on a line or sail. *-adv.* The condition of a line or sail under no load.

slack bilge A displacement hull shape with a continuous curve from the gunwales to the keel.

slack tide The period when there is no horizontal motion of the water at high or low tide.

sling (slĭng) *n.* A fabric strap suspended from lines at each end and used to lift or support a load. See BOSUN'S CHAIR, TRAPEZE, TRAVEL LIFT.

slip (slĭp) *n.* A space at a dock for a vessel; a berth.

slip line A doubled (dock) line with both ends made fast on board.

sloop (sloop) *n.* A single-masted sailboat with a single headsail set from the forestay.

slot (slôt) *n.* The air space between a foresail and the mainsail.

smack (smăk) *n.* A sloop-rigged fishing boat.

small stuff Twine or small-diameter cordage used for whipping and siezing lines.

snatch block A block with a hinged, opening cheek to allow a standing line to be reeved to it.

snub (snŭb) *v.* To check or brake the deployment of a line using the friction of one or more turns around a bitt or cleat.

sole (sōl) *n.* 1. The floor of a cabin or cockpit. 2. A flatfish similar to a flounder.

SONAR (sō'när) *n.* An electronic system which uses transmitted and reflected sound to detect and locate submerged objects or determine water depth.

sound (sound) *v.* To determine water depth. See LEAD LINE, FATHOMETER and TRANSDUCER.

spar (spär) *n.* A pole used as a boom, yard, bowsprit or mast.

spar buoy A mooring buoy made from a short pole. (*also called a* spindle buoy)

spindle (spīn'd-l) *n.* 1. A vertical pole, often set with a daymark, used to mark a hazard to navigation. 2. A mooring buoy made from a short pole. (*also called a* spar buoy)

spinnaker (spīn'ë-kër) *n.* A large triangular sail set on a spar opposite the mainsail when running before the wind.

spinnaker guy A line attached to the outer end of a spinnaker pole.

spinnaker pole A spar attached to the mast and used to control the position of the lower, outer corner of a spinnaker.

spit (spĭt) *n.* A narrow projection of land.

splashboard (splăsh'bôrd) *n.* A shield to keep spray off the deck of a vessel.; a coaming.

splice (splīs) *n.* A joint between two lines formed by interweaving their respective strands.

sponson (spôn'sën) *n.* A structure, such as a gun platform, which protrudes from the side of a vessel.

spoon bow A bow shape with a straight or concave section running aft before flaring out (*as viewed from above*).

spray knocker A horizontal rail attached to or molded into a bow just above the water line to deflect bow spray outward.

spray rail See SPRAY KNOCKER.

spreader (sprĕd'ër) *n.* 1. A crosspiece mounted on a mast used to spread the shrouds away from it. 2. An athwartships rail set above the deck as a mount for lights or other gear.

spring line A dock line other than the bow or stern line, leading forward or aft from its cleat.

spring tide An extreme, astronomical tide, higher than Mean High Water, occurring near a full moon and when the sun, moon and earth are approximately aligned.

spume (spy<u>oo</u>m) *n.* Foam, froth or scum on the water.

squall line A line of potentially violent local storms at the leading edge of a weather front.

SSB See SINGLE SIDE BAND.

stabilizer (stā'bë-lī'zër) *n.* 1. A device affixed to a displacement hull to minimize rolling. 2. An additive to preserve the volatility of fuel during extended storage.

stanchion (stăn'chën) *n.* An upright support for a railing or other equipment.

stand-on Describing a vessel which is expected or required to maintain its speed and course during a maneuver which involves another vessel. Compare GIVE-WAY.

standing part 1. The section of a line not used as part of a knot. 2. The part of a line in a block and tackle that remains stationary with respect to the load.

standing rigging Permanent rigging aloft such as stays and shrouds.

starboard (stär'bërd, ëb'd) *n.* The right side of a vessel when facing forward. *-adj.* On the right side. *-adv.* To or toward the right side.

station (stā'shën) *n.* 1. A specific position aboard, such as the helm station. 2. A specific duty area for a vessel at sea.

statute mile A measure of distance equal to 5,280 feet (*used on-shore*). Compare NAUTICAL MILE.

stave (stāv) *v.* To crush in (*said of a hull*).

stay (stā) *n.* A structural line or cable stretched forward or aft from the top of the mast, part of the standing rigging. See FORESTAY and BACKSTAY.

staysail (stā'sāl or -sël) *n.* 1. A triangular sail set on a stay. 2. The after headsail on a cutter.

steadying sail A small, fore-and-aft rigged sail, set high on a vessel's superstructure to counteract rolling or keep it headed into the wind.

steerageway (stîr'ëj-wā') *n.* Sufficient water passing a rudder to provide directional control.

stem (stĕm) *n.* The vertical extension of the keel that defines the shape of the bow as viewed from the side.

stemhead (stĕm'hĕd) *n.* That part of the stem which protrudes above the sheer line, often notched or fitted with a normanpin for use as a mooring bitt.

step (stĕp) *n.* The socket or block in which the heel of a mast is installed. *-v.* To place a mast in its step. See TABERNACLE.

stepped hull A hull with one or more after sections recessed upward to reduce drag while planing.

stern (stûrn) *n.* The aft section of a vessel.

stern drive An arrangement where the power from an aft-mounted engine is directly transmitted through the transom to an articulated outdrive unit on which the propeller is mounted. See Figure 26.

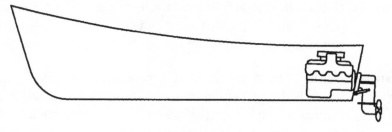

Figure 26

Stern Drive, I/O, Inboard/Outboard

stern line A dock line made fast to an aft cleat.

stern post The main structural member at the stern of a wooden vessel, usually supporting the rudder post.

sternson (stûrn'sĕn) *n.* A structural member set between the keelson and the stern post to reinforce the joint between them. (*also called the* stern knee)

stiff (stĭf) *adj.* Able to carry a large sail (area) without excessive heeling. Compare TENDER.

stock (stŏk) *n.* The cross member nearest the ring or eye of a Navy or Yachtsman's anchor.

stopper knot A knot placed in a line to prevent it from running through an eye or other fitting.

stores (stôrz) *n.* The food and supplies carried on a vessel.

storm anchor A submerged drag, usually fabric over a conical frame, with a line made fast to a bitt, used to keep a vessel headed into heavy weather. (*Also* sea anchor)

storm sails Sails of reduced area for use in heavy weather.

stow (stō) *v.* To replace or store away, especially in an orderly manner.

strake (strāk) *n.* 1. A longitudinal plank of a hull. 2. One of the ridges in a molded hull that simulate lapstrake construction.

stressed skin The outer layer of a structure, such as a hull, which is designed to carry most of the loads applied to it instead of relying on the strength of internal framework (*called* monocoque construction *in aircraft and automotive use*).

stringer (strīng'ër) *n.* A longitudinal structural member of a hull.

stroke oar The set of oars closest to the stern.

strut (strŭt) *n.* 1. A hanger, containing the cutlass bearing, which supports an extended propeller shaft. 2. Any rigid support rod or hanger.

stuffing box A device which uses one or more packing glands to seal the junction where a rotating shaft enters or exits a liquid, especially the passage of a propeller shaft through a hull.

sundeck motor yacht A sedan cruiser with an open deck aft of the flybridge.

superstructure (soop'ër-strŭk'chër) *n.* Any part of a vessel, excluding rigging, that extends above the main deck.

surface-piercing Pertaining to a propeller designed to operate with its upper portion out of the water so that its blades enter the water only on the driving portion of their rotation .

swage (swāj) *n.* A mechanical attachment made by collapsing the walls of a tube or sleeve down onto a cable or shaft under great pressure. -*v.* To make such an attachment.

swamp (swômp) *v.* To overwhelm a vessel with water, causing it to founder.

swamp boat An open, flat-bottomed boat propelled by an engine-driven aircraft propeller mounted above the waterline. (*also called an* airboat)

swell (swĕl) *n.* A gently rising and falling wave that moves without breaking.

swim platform A low, wide platform attached to or molded into the transom and equipped with a ladder to make it easier for swimmers to come aboard.

swing keel A weighted extension of a keel that can be lowered or raised while under way.

T

tab (tăb) *n.* A flap or control surface. See TRIM TABS. *-v.* To use resin-soaked fiberglass strips to bond a bulkhead or other structural member into a hull.

tabernacle (tăb'ër-năk'ël) *n.* A fixture which locates the heel of a mast. See STEP.

tack (tăk) *n.* 1. The position of a vessel relative to the trim of its sails. 2. A line used to secure the forward, lower corner of a fore-and-aft sail. *-v.* 1. To bring a vessel into the wind in order to change its tack. 2. To change the tack of a vessel.

tackle (tăk'ël) *n.* 1. A purchase system using ropes and blocks for mechical advantage. 2. The equipment required for fishing. See GROUND TACKLE.

taffrail (tăf'rāl) *n.* 1. A rail around the stern of a boat. 2. The upper, flat part of the stern of a wooden vessel.

tamarack (tăm'ë-răk) *n.* North American larch tree (*Larix laricina*) valued by wooden boat builders for its strong, fiberous wood, especially for deck-support knees. (*also called* hackmatack)

tang (tăng) *n.* 1. A fitting on a spar for the attachment of standing rigging. 2. A blade-shaped attachment point.

TD Time difference. See LORAN.

teak (tēk) *n.* The wood of a tall evergreen tree (*Tectona grandis*) native to southeast Asia and valued by boatbuilders for its durability.

telltale (tĕl'tāl) *n.* A strip of fabric placed to detect and indicate air motion or wind direction.

tender[(1)] (tĕn'dër) *n.* A small vessel used to service a larger one.

tender[(2)] (tĕn'dër) *adj.* Unable to carry large amounts of sail without heeling excessively. Compare STIFF.

tether (tĕth'ër) *n.* A line or other device that limits the range of motion of the object to which it's attached.

thimble (thīm'bël) *n.* A metal or plastic loop, concave in cross-section, inserted into the eye of a line to protect it from chafing.

thole (thōl) (*also* thole pin) *n.* A pin or set of pins set into the gunwale and used as oarlocks.

through-bolted Attached by fasteners which extend completely through a panel or bulkhead and are secured from the back side.

through hull (also thru hull) Describing any fitting that mounts in an open hole in the hull. Compare SEACOCK.

thwart (thwärt) *n.* A seat across the gunwales of a boat. See ATHWART.

tidal range The difference in depth between Mean High Water and Mean Low Water.

tiller (tĭl'ĕr) *n.* A lever attached to the rudder or rudder post, used to steer the vessel.

toe rail A rail or recess at the perimeter of a cockpit or edge of a deck.

toggle (tôg'ĕl) *n.* 1. A universal joint used to align standing rigging hardware. 2. An auxiliary float used to keep excess lobster trap line from fouling the trap in areas of high tidal ranges.

topgallant (tĕ-găl'ĕnt) *adj.* 1. Describing the mast above the topmast or its sails. 2. Describing the fourth sail from the deck on a square-rigged mast.

topping lift A halyard used to hoist a spinnaker pole.

topsides (tôp'sĭds) *n.* The portion of the hull above the waterline.

tower See TUNA TOWER.

tracking error Deviation from an intended course caused by beam wind or currents. See LEEWAY.

transceiver (trăn'sē'vĕr) *n.* An electronic device capable of transmitting and receiving radio signals.

transducer (trăns'doo'sĕr) *n.* A piezo-electric device which produces and transmits sound waves in a sonar or depth-sounding system.

transom (trăn'sĕm) *n.* 1. The stern of a square-sterned boat. 2. A transverse beam affixed to the sternpost of a wooden vessel.

trapeze (tră'pēz) *n.* A sling suspended from aloft to support crew while hiking out.

travel lift A four-wheeled, self-propelled gantry fitted with slings to lift and transport vessels during hauling or launching.

traveler (trăv'ĕ-lĕr) *n.* An attachment point for sheets or tackle which slides or rolls in a track to provide adjustment or mechanical advantage.

trawler (trôl'ĕr) *n.* 1. A large, comfortable, seaworthy vessel for economical extended cruising, usually with a displacement hull and often with a single engine. 2. A commercial fishing vessel.

tri-hull (trī'hŭl) *n.* 1. A cathedral hull. 2. A trimaran. See Figure 27.

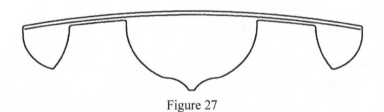

Figure 27

Trimaran

trim (trĭm) *n.* 1. The attitude of a vessel with respect to horizontal or the position of its sails while under way. 2. The general appearance or condition of a vessel. *-v.* To adjust or align to bring into trim.

trim angle 1. The difference between level and the fore-to-aft axis of a vessel at a given speed. 2. The difference between axis of the propeller shaft of an outdrive or outboard motor and the fore-to-aft axis of the vessel.

trim tabs Hydraulically adjustable planing surfaces mounted to the hull below the transom, used to adjust the horizontal attitude of a vessel while under way to compensate for various load , speed and sea conditions. See Figure 28.

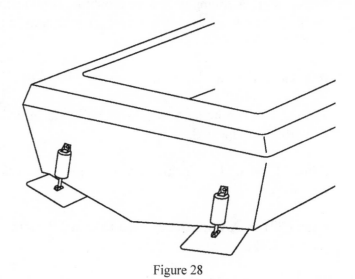

Figure 28

Trim Tabs

trimaran (trī'më-răn) *n.* 1. A boat with three separate hulls. 2. A boat with a single hull and two outriggers.

trip (trīp) *v.* To dip the bow into the water while under way.

trip line A small-diameter line attached to the crown of an anchor to help free it if it becomes fouled on the bottom.

troll (trōl) *v.* To fish by pulling a baited line slowly through the water.

trolling motor A small motor, often electrically powered, used to propel a boat slowly while fishing.

trolling valve A device which enables a vessel's transmission to slip, allowing the vessel to be operated at lower-than-normal speeds using its main propulsion.

truck (trŭk) *n.* 1. A rolling or sliding mounting or attachment point. 2. The block and tackle at the top of a mast used to raise the sails.

true North Geographical North. See MAGNETIC NORTH.

trunk (trŭnk) *n.* The hollow, longitudal bulkhead in which a centerboard is located.

trunk cabin A squared cabin structure which protrudes above the deck.

trunnel (trŭn'ël) *n.* A wooden peg used to fasten the structural members of a wooden boat.

tumblehome (tŭm'bël-hōm') *n.* An inward curvature of the topsides at the top of the transom.

tuna tower A metal tubular structure above the cockpit or cabin which is used as a lookout and helm station.

tunnel drive An arrangement which positions the propulsion mechanism in a tunnel recessed into the hull to reduce draft and protect the propeller.

turn (tûrn) *n.* A single loop of a line around an object.

turn of the bilge The curvature of a displacement or semi-displacement hull where its topsides meet its bottom; a round chine.

turnbuckle (tûrn'bŭk'ĕl) *n.* A device with eyes or other attachment points oppositely threaded into its ends so it may be used to adjust the tension in standing rigging.

turning block A block used to change the direction of a sheet or line.

twin screw Having two engines and propellers.

twing (twîng) *n.* A line used to control the position of another line or guy.

U

umiak (oo'mē-ăk') *n.* An Eskimo boat constructed of animal skins stretched over a wooden frame.

under way In purposeful motion. (*Said of a vessel.*)

undertow (ŭn'dër'tōw) *n.* The outgoing current created by surf retreating from a steep shore. (*also called a* rip current)

unstayed mast (Also **freestanding rig**) A self-supporting mast.

upper shrouds Shrouds which attach to the masthead. Compare LOWER SHROUDS.

V

V berth Sleeping accommodations in the bow of a vessel.

V bottom The shape of a hull, as viewed from astern, where the bottom angles upward from the keel to the chines.

V drive 1. A gearbox whose input and output are on the same end, the output being angled downward and connected to the propeller shaft, which runs aft under the motor. 2. A system which uses such a gearbox. See Figure 29.

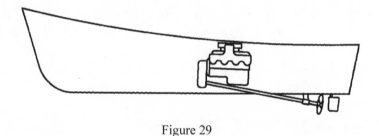

Figure 29

V Drive

vacuum-bagging A manufacturing process which enhances resin infusion into a laminate and reduces the emission of hazardous fumes by enclosing a hull or other molded structure in a plastic bag and applying a vacuum while its resin component is curing.

vang (văng) *n.* A line or tackle running down from a spar or boom to the mast; used to apply tension to the sail.

variation (vār'ē-ā'shën) *n.* The directional difference between true North and magnetic North at a given location.

veer (vēr) *v.* 1. To turn aside from a course. 2. To change direction clockwise (*said of the wind*). Compare BACK.

velocity made good (**VMG**) The true distance over the bottom traveled while under way.

ventilation (věn'të-lā'shën) *n.* 1. The unintended introduction of air or exhaust fumes into the water ahead of a propeller, causing a reduction in its performance. 2. The exchange of air in a closed compartment.

very high frequency (**VHF**) The band of the electromagnetic spectrum used for marine radio communications (*approximately 156 to 164 megahertz [MHz]*).

vessel (věs'ël) *n.* A boat or ship; (*The term is used without regard to length, usually in a legal or technical sense.*)

VHF 1. See VERY HIGH FREQUENCY. 2. A VHF radio transceiver.

VMG See VELOCITY MADE GOOD.

W

wake (wāk) *n.* The disturbance of the water caused by a vessel under way. See BOW WAVE and WASH.

wale (wāl) *n.* 1. A gunwale. 2. A longitudal plank or strake in a vessel's hull.

walk-around A small boat whose cabin is surrounded by a walkway, usually recessed into the deck.

warp (wärp, wôrp) *v.* 1. To move a docked vessel by hauling on its lines. 2. To move a vessel by hauling on the rode of a set anchor. See KEDGE.

wash (wôsh) *n.* The disturbed water left directly behind a boat under way.

washboard (wäsh'bôrd) *n.* (*usually plural*, washboards) Removeable cover(s) for the vertical opening of a companionway.

washdown (wôsh'doun) *n.* An onboard plumbing system for pressurized raw or fresh water, with an outlet in the cockpit or on deck.

watch (wätch) *n.* 1. A period of responsibility for the operation or safety of a vessel. 2. A duty period.

waterline (wä'tër-līn') *n.* The intersection of a vessel's hull and the water's surface.

wave height The vertical distance between the top of a wave and the bottom of its trough.

wave length The horizontal distance between successive waves.

way[1] (wā) *n.* Purposeful motion. (*underway*)

way[2] (wā) *(usually pl.,* **ways)** (wāz) *n.* 1. Rails or guides on which an object may be slid or wheeled. 2. A marine railway used for launching and hauling vessels.

waypoint (wā'point) *n.* A navigational position along a course.

weather deck The horizontal covering which encloses a hull.

weather FAX A service which transmits meteorological charts and weather information by facsimile.

weather radio A report of local weather conditions broadcast on VHF by the National Weather Service.

weather tide A tide running against the wind. Compare LEE TIDE.

well (wĕl) *n.* 1. A berth or slip between fingers or piers. 2. A recess in a deck or sole used for storage of bait or catch.

well-found Well equipped.

whaleboat See LONGBOAT.

wharf (wärf) *n.* A structure, parallel to the shore, to which a vessel may tie up. Compare PIER.

wheel (hwēl) *n.* 1. A vessel's steering wheel. 2. The helm. 3. A propeller.

wheelhouse (hwēl'hous) *n.* An enclosed on-deck cabin containing the helm station.

wherry (hwĕr'ē) *n.* A long, narrow rowboat with a raised stern.

whipping (hwīp'pīng) *n.* Small-diameter cord or twine wrapped around the end of a line to prevent unraveling. -*v.* To wrap the end of a line. See SEIZE.

whisker pole A spar or boom used to support the clew of a genoa away from the boat.

white lead A white, toxic, lead-based compound used in paints and caulking. (Outlawed as a paint additive in the 1960's.)

wide open throttle (WOT) Running a vessel's motor as fast as its condition, installation and operating conditions allow.

winch (wīnch) *n.* A horizontal hand- or power-driven drum around which a line or chain may be wrapped to move a load. See CAPSTAN and WINDLASS.

wind vane A pivoting airfoil which indicates wind direction.

windlass (wīnd'lĕs) *n.* A motor-powered winch or capstan used to haul an anchor.

windward (wīnd'wĕrd) *n.* The direction from which the wind blows. -*adj.* Of or from the side exposed to the wind. -*adv.* Toward or into the wind.

work boat A commercial vessel equipped to service other vessels or equipment.

working part 1. The load-bearing part of a line. 2. The moving part of a line in a block and tackle.

WOT See WIDE OPEN THROTTLE.

Y

yacht (yŏt) *n.* A large pleasure boat with luxurious accommodations.

yacht condition Maintained to very high standards. Bristol.

yacht fisher (*also* **yacht fish** *or* **yacht fisherman**) An aft-cabin or extended-deck cruiser with a small fishing cockpit at the stern.

yankee (yăn'kē) *n.* The forward headsail on a cutter.

yard (yärd) *n.* Horizontal spar from which a square sail is suspended.

yardarm (yärd'ärm) *n.* An extension to a yard.

yaw (yô) *v.* To swing or veer off-course.

yawl (yôl) *n.* A two-masted, fore-and-aft-rigged sailing vessel with a shorter mizzen mast set aft of the rudder post. Compare KETCH.

Z

Zamag (*or* **Zamak**) Trademarks for a lightweight alloy of zinc, aluminum and magnesium, often used for casting marine fittings.

zinc (zīnk) *n.* 1. A soft, blue-white metal used to make sacrificial anodes. 2. A sacrificial anode.

Books published by
Bristol Fashion Publications
Free catalog, phone 1-800-478-7147

Boat Repair Made Easy — Haul Out
Written By John P. Kaufman

Boat Repair Made Easy — Finishes
Written By John P. Kaufman

Boat Repair Made Easy — Systems
Written By John P. Kaufman

Boat Repair Made Easy — Engines
Written By John P. Kaufman

Standard Ship's Log
Designed By John P. Kaufman

Large Ship's Log
Designed By John P. Kaufman

Custom Ship's Log
Designed By John P. Kaufman

Designing Power & Sail
Written By Arthur Edmunds

Building A Fiberglass Boat
Written By Arthur Edmunds

Buying A Great Boat
Written By Arthur Edmunds

Boater's Book of Nautical Terms
Written By David S. Yetman

Practical Seamanship
Written By David S. Yetman

Captain Jack's Basic Navigation
Written By Jack I. Davis

Creating Comfort Afloat
Written By Janet Groene

Living Aboard
Written By Janet Groene

Racing The Ice To Cape Horn
Written By Frank Guernsey & Cy Zoerner

Marine Weather Forecasting
Written By J. Frank Brumbaugh

Complete Guide To Gasoline Marine Engines
Written By John Fleming

Complete Guide To Outboard Engines
Written By John Fleming

Complete Guide To Diesel Marine Engines
Written By John Fleming

Trouble Shooting Gasoline Marine Engines
Written By John Fleming

Trailer Boats
Written By Alex Zidock

Skipper's Handbook
Written By Robert S. Grossman

White Squall - The Last Voyage Of Albatross
Written By Richard E. Langford

Cruising South
What to Expect Along The ICW
Written By Joan Healy

Electronics Aboard
Written By Stephen Fishman

Five Against The Sea
A True Story of Courage & Survival
Written By Ron Arias

Scuttlebutt
Seafaring History & Lore
Written By Captain John Guest USCG Ret.

Cruising The South Pacific
Written By Douglas Austin

Catch of The Day
How To Catch, Clean & Cook It
Written By Carla Johnson

VHF Marine Radio Handbook
Written By Mike Whitehead

REVIEWS

Power & Motoryacht Magazine February 1999

What started as a list for David's own use eventually grew to become *The Boater's Book of Nautical Terms*. The book's contents are alphabetically arranged and terms are clarified with word meaning plus tips on usage and phonetic pronunciation. Appropriately "climate controlled", the book was manufactured to withstand life on a boat. A handy compendium.

Lakeland Boating Magazine December 1998

Say What Sailor?

Dave Yetman's *The Boater's Book of Nautical Terms* provides a handy reference to the unique language that has been developed by the boating community over the years. With more than 1,000 terms and phrases, precise pronunciations and useful illustrations, this book is an ideal resource for new boaters and old salts alike. Boating magazines and dockside conversation will be much less confounding after reviewing the entries in the book.

About The Author

Dave Yetman is a lifelong New Englander who's spent most of his adult life within sight of the water and comes by his nautical interests quite naturally. His seafaring ancestors include Labrador fishermen and lighthouse keepers and a Cape Cod grandfather who was an inventor and shipbuilder and noted for his models of historic New England lighthouses.

His own career has been in mechanical design and engineering, first as an entrepreneur and later as an engineering manager for an international technology company. He's been awarded patents for a wide range of devices, from motorcycle frames to biomedical laboratory instruments and enjoys applying his talents to his boats, which usually end up in a highly customized state.

His work has been widely published in the boating press and was recognized with awards in the 1997 and 1999 Boating Writers International writing competition. His articles, photography and technical illustrations have been published in *Boating World, Lakeland Boating, Motorboating, Offshore, Power & Motoryacht, Sail, Soundings, Trailer Boats* and *Yachting* magazines. He has three books to his credit, "The Boaters' Book of Nautical Terms", "Modern Boatworks" and "Practical Seamanship".

Dave and his wife, Pat enjoy cruising the New England coast on *CURMUDGEON*, their Albin Tournament Express convertible.

CPSIA information can be obtained
at www.ICGtesting.com
Printed in the USA
LVHW111140301122
734324LV00005B/192

9 781892 216113